American Monster

American Monster

The Search for the Sunset Killer

J.T. Hunter

Pedialaw Press

COPYRIGHT

Cover design, formatting and layout by Evening Sky Publishing Services

Library of Congress Control Number:

Printed in the United States of America

Paperback ISBN-13: 978-0-578-28701-0
eBook ISBN-13: 978-0-578-28703-4

AUTHOR'S NOTE

Out of respect for their privacy, the names of surviving victims were changed in this story.

CONTENTS

PART III

In that day, the Lord will punish with his sword,
his fierce, great and powerful sword,
Leviathan the gliding serpent,
Leviathan the coiling serpent.
He will slay the monster of the sea.

– Isaiah 27:1, NIV

PROLOGUE

Her body could not have been there for long. Although it was a cool November night, the young woman's neck still felt slightly warm.

On November 27, 1990, Paul Shannon and his friend, Rickie Sajak, had enjoyed a normal Tuesday night of competing in their weekly bowling league. The two middle-aged men left Forum Lanes in Tamarac, Florida, at nearly midnight, still feeling good about their bowling scores for the evening. True to their usual routine, they decided to do some bass fishing on the way home. They stopped at the usual spot: a canal about a block away from Sajak's house in the middle-class West Glen subdivision. They always enjoyed the quiet, peaceful atmosphere of fishing so late at night.

After about half an hour without any nibbles, the two men

packed up their gear and continued driving through the neighborhood of three and four-bedroom houses in the southwest part of Coral Springs. The route to Sajak's house required them to pass through an area nearly pitch black due to the lack of streetlights around.

As Shannon turned onto the 200 block of NW 122 Avenue, the woman's body appeared out of the darkness. Both men's hearts raced as the beams of their car's headlights revealed the frightening sight.

The young female was nude and lying face down on the shoulder of the street next to a stop sign just north of NW 2nd Street. She was hunched over the curb on 122nd Avenue, bent over in a "doggie style" position, with her head facing west toward a house and her feet in the street.

Having worked in emergency rooms for most of his life, Shannon did not hesitate. He stopped the car, flung the driver's door open, and raced over to help the woman. As he hurried toward her, Shannon hoped that she was merely drunk and passed out.

When he reached her and gently rolled her over, Shannon could see that the woman was in bad shape. Her left eye was open, but it stayed fixed as if staring, while her right eye was completely closed. Shannon checked her neck and wrist for a pulse.

Nothing.

He could see ligature marks on both of the woman's wrists and on both of her ankles. Pieces of brown packing tape were stuck in her hair, suggesting that at some point prior to Shannon's arrival her mouth had been covered by the tape. He saw bruises on her left hand, leg, and knee, and blood on her face appeared to have streamed from her nose.

At 12:51 a.m. Shannon called the Coral Springs Police Department to report the gruesome discovery.

CSPD: Ok, reference that injury that you just called in, ok, you're at 202 NW 122 Ave?

Shannon: Right.

CSPD: Ok, reference to female, what exactly is the problem? Is she unconscious, or what?

Shannon: She may be unconscious, but um, I'm pretty sure she's not. I've moved her around. I tried to get a pulse. Her neck is still warm, but ah, her eyes look fixed, I can't see because there is not enough light here, but I can't find a pulse in her neck or on her wrist, and she looks like a young female. She's naked and looks like someone threw her on the corner here. She was kind of head down, rear end up, and I moved her around, and I just covered her up.

CSPD: Ok, she's right outside in the roadway right now?

Shannon: Right on the corner. I was dropping a friend of mine off, and she, somebody drove by and dumped her there, and ah, if she's not dead, she's almost dead. I'm pretty sure she's dead.

During a subsequent interview with detectives, Shannon elaborated about the condition of the woman's body when he found it.

The only thing that I found unusual was the position of the body. The body appeared to me not to be in a position that ah, of a body that was limp and pushed out of a car. It appeared that someone propped the body in a semi-sexual looking position, with the head down, and the buttocks up, half on the curb, and half off of the curb.

The victim was subsequently identified as 20-year-old Ivelisse Berrios Beguerisse, a student at Broward Community College who lived in nearby Davie.

～

At 10:20 p.m. the night before, Ivelisse – known as "Evi" to her friends – had walked to her car in the parking lot of the Sawgrass Mills Mall in Sunrise, Florida. Her friend and co-worker, Tracy Weaver, accompanied her. The two had worked the evening shift together at the Swim 'N' Sport Outlet, a swimwear store, until it closed at 10:00 p.m. Following regular closing procedures during a "routine evening" with "nothing out of the ordinary," Tracy had vacuumed the store and Evi mopped the floors. After cleaning up, the two locked the front gate of the store at 10:15 p.m. and then walked to the parking lot.

A "quiet, soft spoken, shy type of girl," Evi had on a pink flowered blouse over a sleeveless white dress that fit snug on her petite frame. As they walked out of the White Seahorse entrance of the mall towards the parking lot, Tracy mentioned to Evi that her car was almost out of gas.

"I don't like the idea of going to a gas station after dark," Tracy said.

"Yeah, me too," Evi agreed.

They walked together a little further before saying good night and heading different directions since Tracy's car was parked to the right of a double row of palm trees and Evi's was located to the left. Although all of the parking lot lights were operating, they were not very bright. Still, it only took a minute or so for Tracy to reach her car. As she inserted her key to unlock the driver's side door, she heard what sounded like voices.

Looking back in the direction of the sound, she saw Evi standing by her car. While Tracy watched, Evi walked from the driver's side of her car to the rear and then opened the trunk. At the same time Evi opened her car's trunk, Tracy noticed a white compact car with its headlights on parked behind Evi's vehicle. Tracy could see someone sitting in the driver's seat of the white car, but she could not make out what the person looked like due to the distance and darkness. Since Evi did not appear to be in any distress, Tracy assumed that the person in the white car was Evi's boyfriend or someone else she knew.

"I wanted to go over and see her," Tracy later explained, "but when I saw his car, I just assumed that she would be okay, and I got in the car and left."

Tracy did not look back as she drove out of the parking lot.

Around the same time that Tracy and Evi were walking to the parking lot, Richard Steele, manager of Sun Shades One, finished closing up his store and walked to the mall's parking lot with some of his employees. After escorting several female employees to their cars outside the White Seahorse mall entrance, Steele headed to his own car. As he approached his vehicle, he saw Evi standing in front of her car talking to a white male with a "slender to medium build" who was wearing blue jeans and white high-top sneakers. Since Evi did not seem to be in any distress, Steele got in his car and drove away.

Evi's husband, 26-year-old Bernando Beguerisse, became worried when she did not get home from work at her normal time of 10:30 p.m.

At 11:00 p.m., he called the Swim 'N' Sport, but no one answered.

At 11:20, he called his friend, Angel Sanchez, who told Bernardo to wait until 11:45 and if he had not heard from Evi by then, they would both go look for her.

At midnight, Angel picked Bernardo up and they drove to the mall, pulling into the parking lot around 12:10 a.m. Bernardo spotted his wife's car, a 1985 blue two door Ford

Tempo, in the South Parking Lot about 150 yards from the White Seahorse entrance to the mall. He immediately noticed that the Tempo's front right tire was flat and assumed Evi had started walking home. He and Angel slowly drove along the route that his wife would most likely have taken to walk home, but did not see her. They returned to the mall at 12:45 a.m. and Bernardo told mall security that his wife was missing.

At 3:00 a.m., he arrived at the Sunrise Police Dept to make a missing person report. He told the police that he had instructed Evi that if she ever had car trouble she should not talk to anyone, but should instead call him or Angel to come get her.

When police inspected Evi's vehicle in the mall parking lot, they found that the sidewalls of both passenger side tires had been intentionally punctured. The punctures appeared to have been made by a knife and measured ¼ to ½ inch in length. Police also discovered that a second vehicle's tires had been slashed in similar fashion as Evi's on the same date and in the same parking lot. The second vehicle, a yellow, two-door 1980 Chevrolet Monza, also belonged to a young female who worked at a store inside the mall. That woman, Lenilce Oliveira, had walked to her car with a male friend. After noticing the punctured tires, they called Lenilce's husband and he picked them up around 11:18 p.m.

Investigators noticed many similarities between Evi and Lenilce. In addition to being females employed at the Sawgrass Mills Mall for less than a month and parking in the same area of the parking lot, both women were of Latin descent, both spoke

Spanish, and both had petite figures of approximately five feet tall and one hundred pounds.

~

A cute girl with matching brown hair and eyes, Evi was born and raised in San Juan, Puerto Rico. When she was 7 years old, her family moved to St. Cloud, Florida, for about seven years, then moved back to Puerto Rico. When she turned 18, she returned to Florida and enrolled in the Art Institute in Fort Lauderdale. She met Bernardo on May 19, 1989. They moved in together in mid-August and married on February 13, 1990, the day before Valentine's Day. He was the first and only man she dated in the United States.

Susie Rosado met Evi at the Art Institute in September 1988 and the two had become close friends. Rosado remembered how much Evi seemed to be in love with Bernardo.

"He was her first love and she was very crazy and head over heels for him and everything," Rosado recalled. "It was almost like a story book. It was almost like Cinderella finds her prince, you know?"

Bernardo's nickname for Evi was "Cheperitta," a Spanish term of affection for his "short girl." He described her as a "quiet and shy girl" who was generally "untrusting of people."

Rosado, who perhaps knew Evi better than anyone, insisted that she would have never willingly gotten into a car with a stranger because she "came from a good family" and had a "good head on her shoulders." At the Art Institute, Evi "dressed conservatively," "got along with everybody" and "always got really good grades."

"She was like everybody's little baby sister," Rosado said. "She was the sweetest person that you would ever know. I mean if you ever encountered anybody like that it's very hard to find. I couldn't believe that something like this would happen to her."

Detective Kostick of the Coral Springs Police Department knew exactly what Rosado meant.

"We can't find one person to say one bad thing about her," Kostick said.

Evi had taken the job at the Swim 'N' Sport near the end of October 1990, and she enjoyed working there more than her prior jobs at Chi Chi's restaurant and Sisino's, a tuxedo store. At Swim 'N' Sport she was considered "caring" and a "good employee." Diana Bekins, who often worked Sunday afternoons and evenings with Evi, described her as "very quiet" and someone who "gave the impression of being shy until you got to talk to her, and then she was very warm and friendly."

During the fall semester in 1990, Evi was taking Psychology and French at Broward Community College in Davie, where she was "quiet and shy" and a "good student."

On November 26, Bernardo dropped her off at the college at 9:00 a.m., then picked her up at 11:00 a.m. and they ran some errands before returning home. After showering and getting dressed, Evi left at 5:20 p.m. for work. She drove their two-door Ford Tempo to Sawgrass Mills Mall to start her usual 6:00 p.m. shift. That was the last time Bernardo saw Evi alive.

~

The medical examiner determined Evi's cause of death to be asphyxiation. Crime lab technicians took swabs from her vagina, mouth, and anus, but no suspect DNA could be recovered. Hoping to stimulate the public's memory and generate new leads in the case, investigators staged a re-enactment of the crime scene on December 10 and aired it on television stations throughout Broward County. After the broadcast failed to generate any solid leads, the swabs from Evi's body were returned to the Coral Springs Police Department for storage.

Coral Springs detectives working the case were frustrated by the way the killer seemed to vanish without a trace.

"If there's any case I think that bothers us the most, it's this one," said Sgt. Bob Kostick. "We're giving it a hundred and ten percent and that's all we can do. We just need that one lucky break . . . we're just running out of people to talk to."

The detectives' frustration was reflected in Susie Rosado's reaction. She could not imagine who would have killed such a kind, but cautious, young woman.

She was the last person in the world that anybody could ever murder. I couldn't believe that something like this would happen to her. I mean there's a lot of careless people out there, and there's a lot of people that probably ask for it, like somebody who's involved in drugs or something, but she's a very clean, conservative. She's like an angel, I mean, nobody would do this if they knew her, you know?

That someone would want to harm such an angelic soul was unimaginable and shocking in and of itself. It was even more terrifying to know that the nameless, faceless monster who did so remained free.

PART I

"[T]he devil hath power / T' assume a pleasing shape"

– Hamlet Act 2, Scene 2

ONE

Summertime in Florida. Beautiful beaches, plenty of sunshine, and an abundance of coastline for fishing, scuba diving, or boating. Add to that the mythic allure of Disney World and it's no surprise that the Sunshine State has long been a favorite destination for tourists from around the country and all over the world.

Consisting of the three major cities of Tampa, Clearwater, and St. Petersburg, the greater Tampa Bay area comprises over 2500 square miles in the southwest part of the state, making it the second largest metropolitan area in Florida. And it has lots of water. Covering an area over 400 square miles, the partly brackish water of Tampa Bay is Florida's largest open-water estuary and sits as an extension of the Gulf of Mexico carved into Florida's west coast, stretching around the boundaries of Hillsborough, Manatee, and Pinellas County.

~

Sunday, June 4, 1989 began as a typical summer day.

Then the bodies bobbed to the surface of the bay.

At 9:20 a.m. on that warm, pleasant morning, Steve Leonardo and his wife were on their boat, *Amber Waves*, sailing through Tampa Bay to the Davis Island Yacht Club on their way back from Key West. At the southern edge of the shipping channel near the Sunshine Skyway Bridge, Leonardo spotted something ahead in the water. As he came closer, he was shocked to see a human body floating face-down in the bay. After noting the latitude and longitude of his location about three miles west of Piney Point, Leonardo dialed his marine radio to channel 16 and contacted the Coast Guard.

In response to Leonardo's call, Coast Guard Officer Robert Shidner and three other crew members arrived at the site about 9:40 a.m. in a nineteen-foot rigid-hulled inflatable watercraft. Shidner and the others pulled up beside the bloated, decomposed body of a petite, white female about 5 feet 4 inches tall, and 100-pounds with medium-length brown hair. Wearing only a peach-colored pullover shirt, her hands were tied tightly together and bound behind her back with white cotton rope. A yellow nylon rope commonly used as anchor rope was tied around both of her ankles. A piece of grey duct tape rested on her chin, apparently having slid down from her mouth after her body swelled during the decomposition process.

As Shidner later described it, the unidentified female had a "horrible look on her face" as if she was still experiencing the moment of a terrifying death. It was a sight that would forever haunt the members of the Coast Guard crew.

The same type of yellow rope that bound the woman's ankles was wound tightly around her neck at one end and attached to something underwater at the other. Due to the sixteen-feet depth of the water at the location, Shidner's crew could not see what the body was tied to beneath the waves. Despite their best efforts including pulling on the rope from different angles, they could not budge or dislodge the underwater object and they had no choice but to cut the rope in order to lift the body into their boat.

As Shidner's crew made their way back to the Coast Guard station, a message came over their radio. Another body had been spotted, less than an hour after the first one. They hoisted the first body onto the dock at the station, then headed back out to respond to the second call.

At 10:10 a.m. Florence Secor and a friend were enjoying the morning sun and sea breeze on Secor's sailboat, *Suzi*, when they came across the second body floating face-down in eighteen feet of water a couple of miles southeast of the St. Petersburg Pier, approximately two miles from where the first body was found. This victim was a little taller than the first, about 5 feet 6 inches, and weighed 110 pounds. She had wavy, long brown hair and wore only a black tank top. Like the first body, her hands had been bound with white rope, but the rope remained tied to only one of her hands. The other hand floated free and a portion of grey duct tape had pulled away from her mouth, as if she had managed to partially escape from her bonds while struggling to survive during the final moments of her life.

Similar to the first body, six to eight feet of yellow anchor rope was fastened around the second victim's neck, but this time the Coast Guard recovered a rectangular concrete block that was attached to the other end of the yellow rope. With two square-shaped hollow spaces, it was the type of block commonly used in house construction and weighed about 35 pounds. The same type of yellow rope bound this victim's legs, just as it had on the first body, and the rope dug deep into the skin just above her ankles evidencing the unknown woman's frantic struggles to free herself.

No sooner had the Coast Guard crew secured the second body in their boat than another call came over the radio. Yet another body had been found. Shidner could not believe it.

One body floating in the bay was bad enough.

Two was horrific.

Three was simply beyond imagination.

At 10:40 a.m., Dale Bollert was heading to Apollo Beach on his boat, *Charlie Girl*, when he saw Shidner's Coast Guard craft in the distance pulling something from the water. As Bollert drew closer he spotted the third body in the water about two hundred yards from the second, floating face-down in the same manner. This victim was the largest of the three: 5 feet 7 inches and 125 pounds. She had long, sandy-colored hair and wore only a black, sleeveless t-shirt. A gold wedding band was on her left ring finger. Her legs were tied with the same type of yellow rope that bound the first two bodies. One end of the rope bound her ankles and the other end was tied to a concrete mason block. Like both of the other two victims, the hands of body number three were bound with white rope and she was nude from the waist down. She had been gagged with the same silver-grey duct tape as the other two victims.

Decomposition, bloating, and skin marbling made it nearly impossible to tell what the three women looked like prior to death. Their bodies resembled something out of a horror movie more than the living human beings they once were. As surgeon Sherwin Nuland observed in *How We Die*, when a drowning victim is found after having been submerged for several days, "it is difficult for its appalled discoverer to believe that this rotted thing once contained a human spirit and shared nature's life-giving air with the rest of healthy humanity."

But as horrifying as the effects of the decomposition process and bloating were, it was those very effects that allowed the crime to be detected at all. The warm water of the bay during the summer enabled putrefaction to produce enough gas in the victims' tissues to make their bodies sufficiently buoyant to rise to the surface.

"The water temperature was hot," said St. Petersburg Police Department Detective Glen Moore. "Had this occurred in much colder temperatures, in much colder water, one cinder block might have held them under the surface."

~

After arriving back at the Bayboro Coast Guard station in St. Petersburg around 12:30 p.m., Shidner's crew arranged three Army Green, tarp body bags on the dock for transport to the Medical Examiner's Office. The Coast Guard also dispatched a team of divers to retrieve whatever had been weighing down the first body, but they were not able to find it.

During the process of recovering the bodies, the Coast Guard crew discovered a 32-foot boat almost fully submerged within 100 feet of the second and third bodies. Believing that the sunken boat could might have some connection with the three bodies, they towed it back to the Coast Guard station as well.

After ending their shift, the Coast Guard crew struggled to deal with what they had experienced. Team member Lori Brandon tried in vain to block out the images of the three dead women.

How terrifying it must have been to die like that, was the thought that kept repeating in her mind.

Robert Shidner was also deeply affected by what he had witnessed.

"We had some nightmares and stuff the first night," he later recalled. "When you see someone as helpless as those three women were . . . and they were tied . . . and the expression of horror on their faces . . . it was pretty rough."

TWO

Since the bodies were found on the St. Petersburg side of the bay, the St. Petersburg Police Department became the lead agency on the case. The brutality of the crimes made it difficult to work the case, even for those in the department who were used to coming into contact with the darker side of human nature.

"I think everybody's been shocked by this, even among cops" homicide Detective Gene Black remarked. "You've got a whole family wiped out, practically. And then the style of death . . ." he added, his voice trailing off.

"It was the most shocking thing I had seen, and probably the most shocking thing anyone had seen in that area," agreed Detective Glen Moore.

"All homicides are serious," said long-time prosecutor

Bernie McCabe, "but the terror that had to be involved in this one is extraordinary."

Beyond the ranks of law enforcement, the monstrous nature of the triple murder horrified and fascinated the residents of the Tampa Bay area. The heinous killing of a mother and her two daughters, so barbaric and cruel, put the community on edge, and the knowledge that the killer remained on the loose left anxious parents fearful that something could happen to their loved ones as well.

"We've got almost nothing to go on," said Sgt. Bill Sanders, head of the St. Petersburg Police Department's homicide unit. He theorized that the victims may have been on vacation or runaways because if they were local someone would likely have come forward to identify them. He added another possibility as well.

"Maybe they're witnesses to some kind of crime," Sanders remarked, speculating about the possibility of a drug-related execution. "We'll never know that until we know who they are."

As a general rule, the first thing detectives do in any murder case is identify the victims, but the nature of the crime scene and manner of disposal of the three bodies in the bay, made that difficult. Having a crime scene on the water posed a particular challenge to investigators since any hair, fibers, fingerprints, semen, or other trace evidence of the crimes had been literally washed away prior to the victims' bodies being discovered.

"Any evidence you have degrades immediately," said Sgt. David Byington. "On land you may have wind, rain, or animals, but in the water, you've got all of that."

In an effort to identify the victims, the police held a news conference on June 5 displaying the jewelry worn by "Jane Doe 1, Jane Doe 2, and Jane Doe 3," hoping that a friend or relative of the victims would recognize it. No one did.

The medical examiner's autopsy results were similar for all three of the victims, listing the cause of death for each as "homicidal violence, asphyxia." Drowning is a form of asphyxia, but the bodies had been in the water for so long, estimated as two to three days, that the telltale signs of drowning could not be utilized. The bodies' advanced state of decomposition was such that the medical examiner could not even determine whether the three women were dead when thrown into the water.

The report about the largest of the three bodies, the third one that had been found, noted yellow rope in a slipknot around the victim's neck with the other end tied to a concrete block, and included the description:

> extremely bloated and exhibits general skin slippage and marbling. The scalp is covered with long blonde hair which is loosely adhered to the scalp. The eye color cannot be determined . . . The chest, abdomen, and back are unremarkable except for decomposition.

To ascertain how the victims' bodies ended up at the locations where they were found, investigators enlisted the aid of Bernard Ross, a civil engineering professor at the University of South Florida with twenty years of experience studying tidal movements in Tampa Bay. Ross used computer models of seawater flow to determine that the three bodies must have been dumped overboard from a boat near the shipping lane in the middle of the bay about 3 to 3 ½ miles from where they were recovered. Due to the swirling, loop-pattern currents in the area where the bodies were found, Ross acknowledged a margin of error of about two miles north or south. Nonetheless, he could say several things for certain.

"They didn't come in from the mouth of the bay, they didn't come off the bridges, and they didn't get dumped off of land," Ross concluded.

In the meantime, after tracking down the owner of the 32-foot boat found nearly fully submerged close to where the bodies were discovered, investigators ruled out the boat as having any connection to the triple homicide. The boat's owner had been forced to abandon the boat on the evening of June 3 when it began leaking while he was testing the seaworthiness of a resurfacing job he had done to the bottom of the boat.

∽

Four days after the bodies were found, police got their first real lead in the case. On June 8, a maid at the Days Inn on Rocky Point Island at 7627 Courtney Campbell Causeway noticed that the two double beds in Room 251 had not been slept in for nearly a week. None of the bathroom towels had been used either. Having read in the newspaper about the three bodies in the bay, she suspected something might be wrong so she notified the motel's General Manager, Sergio Ortiz.

When Ortiz inspected Room 251 to check for himself on what the maid had reported, he saw swimming suits, suntan lotion, food, and pieces of luggage scattered around the room. A white-and-blue Igloo cooler sitting on the floor at the foot of the first bed contained spoiled food. After viewing the condition of the room, Ortiz contacted the Tampa Police Department.

Officer Mitchell Wilkens responded to the motel around 11:40 a.m. Ortiz explained to him that three women believed to be a mother and two daughters had checked into Room 251 a week earlier on June 1, but their room did not appear to have been used and they had not been seen by motel staff since that time. The mother and two daughters were supposed to have checked out several days earlier, but failed to do so.

When Wilkens inspected the room, he found it to be a standard, low-frills, double-bed room with dark blue carpet. Curtains on the window matched the blue bed spreads. A large, orange suitcase, still filled with clothes, sat open on the floor next to a grey duffle bag. A black tote bag had been tossed onto an end table in a corner of the room along with several beach towels. Rolls of camera film, some opened and some unopened, were scattered on top of the TV and the dresser beside it. Two blue chairs were arranged next to the wall air conditioning unit and a plastic Disney World bag prominently displaying Mickey Mouse had been placed on one of the chairs. A pair of women's white tennis shoes were on the ground next to the other chair.

Although some clothes had been tossed onto one of the beds, both of the blue bed spreads with pink flower patterns were still neatly made.

A review of the front desk records revealed that Joan Rogers of Willshire, Ohio, had checked herself and her two daughters into Room 251 seven days earlier. The registration included the make, model, and license tag of the Rogers' car, but the car was nowhere to be found in the motel's parking lot. Patrol officers drove opposite routes from the motel searching in both directions of the Courtney Campbell Causeway looking for Joan Rogers's vehicle, a blue two-door 1986 Oldsmobile Cutlass Calais with Ohio license plate 230-TCU. They found it in the parking lot of a public boat ramp right off the causeway two miles away from the Days Inn, roughly 25 miles from where the three bodies had been discovered a week earlier.

The car was locked and facing the water. A map lay on the left rear passenger seat along with a cardboard sun-shade that displayed "Need Help. Please Call Police" when fully unfolded. The front passenger seat was leaning forward consistent with someone having exited from the back seat, supporting the conclusion that at least three people had been in the car when it was parked.

An 8 ½ by 11-inch piece of Days Inn Rocky Point Island stationary lay on the front seat with the handwritten note:

turn rt (w on 60) – 2 1/2 mi – on rt side alt before bridge
blue w/wht

Those directions accurately reflected the drive down the Courtney Campbell Causeway (Highway 60) from the Days Inn, with the boat ramp parking lot located to the right of the last light before the causeway becomes a bridge. A tourist brochure advertising Clearwater Beach lay amongst various other items, including a deck of Uno cards and a puzzle book. An air-freshener printed with the words "Born to Party" dangled from the rear-view mirror.

"We're going to be working diligently to confirm or deny that the people who stayed in that room are in fact the people that we pulled out of the bay," said St. Petersburg Deputy Chief Hal Robbins.

As part of that diligence, technicians at the Tampa Police Department's lab developed the film found in Room 251. Most of the photographs were from the attractions the Rogers had visited, and included shots of giraffes, parrots, monkeys, and lions at the Jacksonville Zoo, as well as Disney characters like King Louie the orangutan and Baloo the Bear from *The Jungle Book*.

One photograph showed the interior of the motel room and another showed Michelle Rogers sitting on the floor wearing a blue bikini top with white Bermuda shorts and sandals. Slightly sunburned on her neck, Michelle faced the camera as if the photographer had disturbed her, the kind of shot that a little sister might take to purposely annoy her older sibling.

The last photo on the last roll of film captured the view from the room's balcony. The camera faced northwest looking across the motel's rear parking lot past a group of palm trees towards the distant water of Tampa Bay, daylight dwindling as the sun began its descent. Based on the position of the sun and shadows, a forensic expert determined that the photo had been taken between 6:30 and 8:00 p.m. Meteorology records showed that the sun had set at 8:22 p.m. on June 1.

The only fingerprints obtained from Room 251 matched those of the three Rogers women, and on June 9, dental records flown in from Ohio confirmed that the three bodies were those of Joan (36), Michelle (17), and Christe (14) Rogers. Having identified the three victims, the St. Petersburg and Tampa Police Department released photos of Joan, Michelle, and Christe along with a joint appeal to the public for help in identifying their killer.

"We've never had a murder like this before," announced Sergeant Bill Sanders. "At this point, we don't have any leads or suspects in mind."

THREE

In Willshire, Ohio, a rural area of Van Wert County on the northwest border of Ohio and Indiana, the town of 500 residents reacted to the murders of Joan, Michelle, and Christe with shock and disbelief.

"This is a small, tight-knit community," said Reverend Gary Luderman, pastor at Zion Lutheran Church. "Everybody knows everybody. We're an extended family and when one person hurts, we all hurt."

Joan's husband, Hal Rogers, had reported her and their two daughters missing on Wednesday, June 7. The three were due home from vacation on Sunday, June 4, and when that day came and went with no word from them, Hal began to worry. He had been looking forward to hearing all about the fun times his wife and two daughters had at Disney World and Busch Gardens.

Instead, on June 9, the Van Wert Sheriff showed up at Hal's door to deliver the news that his entire family had been brutally murdered. Their bound and bloated bodies had been fished out of the waters of Tampa Bay on the very day that Hal expected to see them pulling into the driveway.

~

High school sweethearts, Hal and Joan – pronounced Jo-Ann – married in nearby Convoy, Ohio on October 16, 1971, four months after Joan's graduation from Crestview High School. The two had a lot in common, not the least of which was the fact that they had both grown up on farms. In fact, both could trace their ancestors back for several generations on Van Wert County farms.

At the same time, the marriage was a true case of opposites attract. Hal, a reserved loner, found what complimented and completed him in Joan, a gregarious extravert who went by "Jo" to those who knew her. While Hal was quiet and introspective, Jo had the kind of outgoing, friendly personality that "never knew a stranger." They had two daughters, Michelle, and Christe, and the four of them lived together in a small, white, one-story home on their dairy farm located on Route 1, Ainsworth Road, a couple of miles outside of Willshire.

Like most of the area's hard-working, church-going residents, the Rogers lived a "Norman Rockwell existence" on their 200-acre farm, just one of many such farms in Van Wert County. Three large grain silos behind the house towered above it, while a large barn sprawled between the silos and house. Although Hal worked long days on the farm, all four family members were usually awake every morning by 5:30 a.m. to help with milking the cows and tending the crops.

The family struggled financially, especially in the beginning, and to make some extra money and get medical insurance, Joan took a job working the midnight shift at Peyton Northern, a food warehouser and distribution center in Bluffton, Indiana, just over the Ohio state line. She had been working there since 1987, operating a forklift to move heavy pallets of goods throughout the night before heading home and helping Hal with the farm.

The trip to Florida had been planned as a vacation for the whole family. However, heavy spring rains kept the fields flooded for too many days and put Hal so far behind planting schedule that he had to stay home to complete a late planting of corn, wheat, and soybeans. Despite all of the work that needed to be done, Hal still wanted his wife and kids to go on the trip because he knew how much Michelle and Christe were looking forward to it. Indeed, Michelle had been meticulously marking the days on a calendar until their departure. So Hal urged them to go enjoy Disney and see whatever else they wanted to see.

Hal's wife and daughters left home at 1:30 p.m. on Friday, May 26. They planned on returning a week later since Joan had to be back by Monday, June 5 to work at Peyton Northern and Michelle needed to make up a Chemistry class in summer school starting on June 5 as well. The Florida vacation was the first overnight trip Michelle and Christe had ever taken out of the state.

"They never got much vacation because of the farming," neighbor Kevin Harmon explained.

"This is the first vacation they ever had, to my understanding," echoed Joe Steffan, a local teacher who knew the family.

Florida was the natural choice for the trip because a substantial number of Van Wert County's retirees spent their winters in the Sunshine State, making it simultaneously familiar and exotic.

"I guess one of the goals we have as parents is to take our families down to the Orlando area and Disney World," Steffan confirmed.

～

Just 5'1" tall, Christe was "a little ball of fire" and made up for what she lacked in height with her large personality. An eighth grader and cheerleader, Christe was "bubbly" and "very outgoing, very social." She looked like her father, but had her mom's outgoing personality.

Michelle, a junior, was "a lot quieter . . . like her father." With brown-hair past her shoulders and brown eyes, she had her mom's looks, but her dad's introverted character. She was a tomboy and "typical farm girl" who enjoyed being involved in her school's 4-H program, and studying biology and zoology. A "down-to-earth, jeans and t-shirt girl," Michelle planned to attend college because she did not want to work the farm her whole life, though she did not rule out becoming a veterinarian one day.

~

On June 13, nearly 300 people attended the funeral services for Joan, Michelle, and Christe at Zion Lutheran Church, a Gothic style building with red-brick walls and green spires in Shumm, Ohio. At Hal's request, a teddy bear had been placed inside each of the three closed caskets and the top of each casket was adorned with white roses. Reverend Luderman included comments in his sermon directed at the question of why God would allow such a terrible thing to happen.

> We've been gathered here before for funerals and we've always asked, 'Where was God?' You may be asking yourself now where was God when Joan, Christe, and Michelle were crying out in pain? Where was God when these terrible things were happening to them in Tampa Bay?

The pastor assured the attendees that God was with the Rogers women in their final moments providing comfort to them.

"God was with them," he said. "They were not going toward death, but toward life."

After the service, church bells rang while friends and neighbors followed three hearses carrying the three coffins across the street into the small Zion Lutheran Church Cemetery. Moving quietly except for the occasional sounds of sobbing, the processional gathered on a grassy knoll for the burial, where Hal Rogers took flowers from a bouquet and handed them one-by-one to his daughters' friends.

Neighbor Martin Ross stood outside his car after the funeral and thought about Christe and Michelle.

"It's a sad situation. I held them in my arms when they were babies," he said. "They played in my yard and helped on my farm. They were wonderful girls. It doesn't make any sense. It doesn't make any sense at all."

When he heard the news about their bodies being found, Jeff Feasby, Michelle's 17-year-old boyfriend, stormed to his truck. He needed to be alone and drove around trying to clear his head. Besides the shock and grief of losing his girlfriend, he felt immense anger towards whoever had killed 14-year-old Christe.

"She was only a little girl," he said. "What kind of person would do that to her?"

Feasby had his own theory about the murderer: "I don't think it was anybody from around here. It was probably just some sick bastard . . . one thing I do know is they would never have gotten on some stranger's boat alone. Never."

Although everyone experiences grief differently, Hal's behavior during the funeral and burial perplexed Reverend Luderman. He knew that Hal tended to keep his emotions bottled up inside, but he found it odd that Hal never wept or broke down during the funeral proceedings or when Luderman undertook his role as grief counselor.

"I never really got the feeling that he was paralyzed by grief," Luderman explained. "I never noticed any great grief at all, I just didn't. I'm sorry to say that, but I didn't."

He remembered seeing Hal standing outside the church one day after Sunday service. Luderman had walked over to Hal and put his hand on the widower's shoulder to offer emotional support.

"Don't ever touch me again, Gary," Rogers had said after brashly pushing the pastor's hand away.

Now the reverend wondered whether Hal had something to hide.

"I don't have any idea what goes on behind those eyes," Luderman remarked. "They look dead. Everything about him is so controlled, so withdrawn. I just don't know what goes on inside that man. I've never experienced anyone like him."

Luderman was not alone in his assessment. Others in town began to wonder about Hal as well. The parents of Michelle's best friend, Holly Coleman, forbid her from visiting Hal at his house after they learned that he had commented how it was going to be strange dating girls his daughters' ages.

"My wife and I said enough and kept Holly from going over there," her father, Bob Coleman, said. "It was just very unhealthy after a point, very strange."

And that was before they learned that Hal called Holly and asked her if she wanted to go out sometime and have a beer with him. For his part, Hal Rogers refused to speculate whether the police considered him a suspect in the deaths of his wife and daughters.

"If I'm a suspect, they're wasting their time because I didn't do it," he asserted. "I don't know if they're going to ever find who did do it, but I don't think about it too much," he explained. "There's nothing I can do."

FOUR

On June 16, using receipts found in Joan Rogers's car and motel room, Detective Ralph Pflieger prepared an itinerary of the Rogers' vacation travels.

Rogers' Vacation Itinerary

Day 1 (May 26) – The three women left their Ohio home at 1:30 p.m. and drove out of town, then headed south on I-75, stopping in Dalton, Georgia at a Best Western where they stayed overnight.

Day 2 (May 27) – The trio continued driving south on I-75 and stopped at a Florida Welcome Center just over the state border in Jennings, then made their way to Jacksonville, Florida, where they stayed overnight in a Day's Inn off I-10.

Day 3 (May 28) – After checking out of their motel around 9:00 a.m., they visited the Jacksonville Zoo. Michelle sent her friend, Lori Jenkins, a postcard showing some of the animals and joked that she had seen a monkey that reminded her of her boyfriend. From the zoo, they drove to Silver Springs outside Ocala. After enjoying a glass-bottom boat ride at Silver Springs, they drove to Titusville and stayed at a Quality Inn in Titusville near the Kennedy Space Center.

Day 4 (May 29) – On the fourth day of the trip, they drove to Orlando and spent the day at Sea World before checking into the Gateway Inn on International Drive late that night. At some point that day, Joan dropped Hal a postcard in the mail with a picture of two vintage cars that were on display at Silver Springs, and Michelle sent a postcard to Jeff Feasby. Both mailings painted a picture of a fun-filled vacation; neither indicated any trouble or concern.

Joan's postcard to Hal read:

Stayed the nite at Titusville. Leaving for Sea World then Disney World tonite for three nites. Weather is hot and humidity is very high (98%). Kids having a great time, dragging me everywhere, seeing Silver Springs. Went on a glass bottom boat ride. Better go, have to get Christe out of bed. Love ya – Take care – don't work too hard.

In her postcard to Feasby, Michelle wrote:

Hi! How is everything with you? I'm doing great. Yesterday we went to the Zoo in Jacksonville. I was visiting my relatives and we found Geoffrey (you). Later we went to Silver Springs and rode on a glass bottom boat. Today we are going to a beach and then to Sea World. You have fun at work and behave yourself. Have a great birthday. I'll be thinking of you! I miss you!

Love ya,
Chelle

Day 5 (May 30) – They spent the next day of their Orlando stay at Epcot Center.

Day 6 (May 31) – For their final day in Orlando, they went to Disney's MGM Studios.

Day 7 (June 1) – Having finished their time at Disney, the three Rogers women drove to Tampa and checked into the Days Inn on Rocky Point Island at 12:28 p.m. Their whereabouts during the afternoon remained a mystery. However, a witness placed them in the motel restaurant around 7:30 p.m.

Witness interviews enabled investigators to flesh out some of the Rogers' movements leading up to their disappearance:

Susan Meadows, Assistant Manager of the Days Inn at Rocky Point, had helped Joan, Michelle, and Christe check in around 12:30 p.m. on June 1. As her mom filled out the registration card, Christe asked about information on area attractions. Meadows handed her a Busch Gardens brochure and told them to wear their bathing suits if they went there since people tended to get wet at the theme park.

At 12:37 p.m. Michelle called her boyfriend, Jeff Feasby, at Global Service Center, the Union 76 automobile service station where he worked in Van Wert. Jeff and Michell had known each other since 7th Grade. They went to junior prom together at Crestview High School, and Jeff had given her his class ring.

During their telephone conversation, Michelle wished Jeff a happy birthday and let him know that they had checked-in at the motel. Michelle talked a lot and sounded "real happy" during the 9-minute call. She told Jeff that they were "having a great time" and mentioned that she wanted to go to the beach and swim, but her mom would not let them go near deep water since they were not very good swimmers.

Phone records also revealed that after settling into their room, Joan called Busch Gardens at 12:57 p.m., perhaps checking on its hours of operation and ticket costs. However, investigators could not place the Rogers women at Busch Gardens that afternoon, or anywhere else for that matter.

At about 7:15 p.m. that night, business traveler Roger Jacobs went to dinner at the Days Inn's restaurant. It was not very crowded and the hostess seated Jacobs at a table beside a row of booths. The three Rogers women were eating directly in front of him in one of them. Michelle sat on one side of the booth and Joan and Christe on the other. They were "laughing and joking in a very good mood" while they ate. Since they were directly across from his line of vision, Jacobs could not help but watch them while he ate his dinner of ribeye steak, baked potato, and carrots. Around 7:40 p.m., when Jacobs was nearly finished eating, the three women got up from the booth and left. As Michelle walked by him, she looked down, smiled, and said "Hi".

Cashier Sylvia McCrary reported seeing the Rogers girls in her convenience store at 825 West Bearss Avenue in Tampa around 11:45 p.m. that night. One of the teenage girls told her that they were on vacation from Ohio and had been to Disney World. However, investigators doubted McCrary's account because it did not fit the probable timeline of the Rogers' disappearance.

～

As mid-June temperatures climbed into the 90's, police handed out fliers at the boat ramp where Joan's car was found, hoping to jar someone's memory. The fliers had photographs of Joan, Michelle, and Christe with "Homicide Bulletin" written above the photos and "Public Assistance Requested" below them.

"We have absolutely nothing to go on," Detective Rick Stanton said as he handed out the fliers. "And we're just hoping someone saw something."

FIVE

Despite reconstructing the Rogers' vacation timeline, viable leads began dwindling two weeks into the investigation of their murders. By June 17, detectives had run down "hundreds of leads," but even the most promising ones ended in dead ends, and investigators' hopes of identifying the killer began to fade.

One of the best leads centered on a blue-and-white boat seen on a trailer attached to a dark-colored Bronco or Blazer in the Day's Inn parking lot on June 1. Another concerned reports of a man in a boat trying to pick up women at the boat ramp where Joan Rogers's car was found. Detectives ultimately ruled out both suspects, but not before expending hundreds of man-hours tracking down the boat by assembling lists of motel employees and guests at each place the Rogers trio stayed and then comparing the lists with the over 700,000 boaters registered in Florida. The investigators working the case grouped the leads into piles numbered one through five, with the stack of fives deemed the highest priority. Now only the lowest priority leads remained.

"It's a very, very frustrating and a very, very difficult case," said Sgt. Bill Sanders, head of the homicide division at the St. Petersburg Police Department. "We don't have any promising information and there is no explanation for what happened. But then, how do you explain a Ted Bundy?"

Sanders's reference to infamous serial killer Ted Bundy proved telling, as the frustrated police departments from Tampa and St. Petersburg sought assistance from the FBI's Behavioral Science Unit in Quantico, Virginia. Since its development during the mid-1970s as a clearinghouse for information on serial killers, the BSU had become famous for its ability to profile and help catch serial killers like Bundy. Although the Rogers' killer was not believed to have crossed state lines to commit the triple homicide, the slayings were deemed "heinous enough" to warrant the FBI's involvement. But because the bodies had been recovered from the waters of Tampa Bay, the lack of a tangible crime scene from which to gather evidence limited the agency's ability to piece together a complete psychological profile of the killer.

On June 18, twelve days after discovery of the Rogers' bodies, *The Tampa Tribune* newspaper featured a story with the headline *Family escaped tragedy in Ohio only to find death in Tampa Bay*. The article detailed homicide experts' bewilderment over how an "average Ohio farm family" could fall victim to violent crime twice in a short period of time. The vacation to Florida had been intended as a reward for Michelle and Christe's good grades in school, but also as an escape for the family, particularly Michelle, from the aftermath of a history of rape by her uncle, 32-year-old John Rogers.

Hal's brother, John, had been arrested in February 1988 and given a 7-to-25-year prison sentence in 1989 pursuant to a plea deal. The plea spared Michelle from testifying at trial, but did not shield her from the trauma of having been sexually assaulted by a trusted family member or from the subsequent investigation of the assaults. Michelle had to relive the trauma in April 1988 when she was interviewed by the Van Wert Sheriff's Department and the Department of Human Services.

A Vietnam War veteran, John Rogers had jointly owned the farm with Hal and lived in a trailer on the farm next door to his brother's family. In November 1987, an eighteen-year-old woman moved into the trailer with him in exchange for paying him rent. On the night of February 14, 1988, he raped her at knifepoint after she returned home from a date. When police arrived to question him about the woman's allegations of rape, they noticed a brown briefcase in the living room, which he claimed contained tax papers. However, a subsequent inspection of the briefcase revealed a videotape of the rape as well as photos of a bound and blindfolded, seminude young woman along with several audiotapes. Although police assumed the photos were of John's accuser, they were actually photographs of his teenaged niece, Michelle. The photos documented just one of the many times he had raped her between June 1, 1986 and November 1987.

Michelle was only 14 when the rapes started. They usually involved her being tied up and blindfolded, sometimes at knife point, and the rapes always occurred when her parents were away from the farm. The first time her uncle raped her happened while she was helping him with a medical issue.

"He had back problems and you had to go over and rub his back down because it would get cramps in it," Michelle explained to detectives in 1988.

As she was rubbing his back "he started rubbing my back and I told him quit it and then my shirt came off and he took my pants off and fucked me."

When her uncle finished, he warned her that he would hurt her if she told anyone. Shocked by what had happened, Michelle took a shower and went to bed. She tried to block out what had happened, but then it happened again.

The second time John Rogers threatened her by holding a knife to her neck, then made her walk to his trailer where he forced her to perform oral sex on him before having intercourse. He repeatedly made her call him "Master" during the rape.

Her uncle raped her six times over the next year and a half. Strangely, Hal Rogers posted the bail to get John out of jail following his arrest for rape. And Hal and John's mother insisted that Michelle had lied to the police about John raping her.

∾

Holly Coleman, Michelle's best friend who she had confided in about the rapes, took the news of the murders particularly hard. Holly had been invited to accompany Michelle on the Florida trip, but her parents declined to let her go. Now she felt guilty for not having been there, as if her presence could have prevented the family from falling victim to a brutal crime within hours of their arrival in the Tampa Bay area.

One of Holly's first thoughts upon learning about the murders was that John Rogers had killed the three Rogers women in revenge for Michelle telling the police about his history of sexually assaulting her. And Holly was not the only one thinking that way. Rumors spread throughout town that John Rogers had something to do with the murders. After all, he had traveled to Florida in February or March 1989, just a few months before the killings, and stayed near Tampa during his six-week visit, making stops in some of the same places his nieces would soon visit, including Disney World, Busch Gardens, and Kennedy Space Center.

Wanting to sever all ties with the man who raped his daughter, Hal bought-out John's share of the farm, so John had plenty of cash to burn during his trip to Florida. But investigators quickly ruled him out as a suspect since he was in prison when the murders occurred and it would have been extraordinarily difficult for him to coordinate a hired killer to murder the three women during their travels.

Despite detectives' assurances that John Rogers was not involved, Coleman remained wary of him. She remembered things that Michelle had shared with her during their conversations about her uncle and the rapes.

"When she first told me," Coleman recalled, "she was very scared of John. He once killed a dog and told her he would do it to her if she told anybody about what was going on." According to Coleman, Michelle also feared her own father, Hal Rogers, because he had a history of violent, sometimes strange, behavior.

"Animals were disappearing or turning up dead on that farm all the time," Coleman explained. "Hal had a horrible temper. Michelle said that he once punched a cow to death with his fist because it did something to him, stepped on him or something."

If Coleman's statements were true, Michelle had more than one reason to want to leave behind small-town life on the farm and escape to Florida, the land of Disney, where dreams come true, even if only for a little while.

SIX

As the calendar turned to July, the investigation stagnated. Leads in the Rogers case came few and far between, and those that seemed promising at first glance inevitably led nowhere. In one such lead, a bouncer at a Tampa strip club telephoned the St. Petersburg Police Department to report that several days after the Rogers' bodies had been found, a "slightly chubby" white male with "reddish-blonde hair" started talking to one of the club's dancers at the bar. Acting "nervously," the man told the dancer that he met some people from Ohio, confiding to her: "I felt bad, because I wanted the young girl so bad, I had to kill the others to get to her."

Another lead that fell through involved a local man who owned a blue and white boat who was seen offering a ride to a couple at the same boat ramp where Joan and the girls had disappeared. The man had a criminal record including burglary, grand theft, and aggravated assault. Police found two concrete blocks on the ground behind his boat and both yellow rope and white rope inside of it. However, the man's alibi held up: on the night of the murders he had been boating with his girlfriend.

By September, the St. Petersburg Police Department disbanded the task force investigating the Rogers murders, reducing the number of detectives working the case from more than two dozen detectives at its high point down to just two, the number routinely assigned to typical homicide cases.

"That's what we're down to now. We really have no place to go," Major Cliff Fouts explained, confirming that unless new information materialized investigators had little hope of finding Joan, Michelle, and Christe's killer.

But something happened the following month that injected new life into the case. In October, while reviewing a statewide law enforcement publication issued monthly by the Florida Department of Law Enforcement, Detective James Kappel read about the rape of a Canadian tourist on a blue and white boat in Madeira Beach, about twelve miles northwest of St. Petersburg. Kappel was stunned to learn that the rape had occurred on May 15, 1989, only two weeks before the Rogers murders. He immediately wondered whether the two cases could be connected.

When Kappel contacted his Madeira Beach colleagues, they advised that they had not informed the St. Petersburg Police Department about the rape case because Madeira Beach detectives were never told details about the Rogers murders. Under police procedures generally followed at the time, the lack of communication between police agencies was more the rule than the exception. The basic explanation was that there had been nothing special about the rape case to cause Madeira Beach investigators to reach out to the St. Petersburg detectives about it.

"A rape case on a boat is not uncommon," said Madeira Beach Sgt. John Remedis. "It's not the first time somebody was raped on a boat."

After reviewing details about the Madeira Beach rape case, Detective Kappel traveled to Canada to interview the victim, Jan Bradley, and her friend, Becky Matthews. Jan, a 25-year-old social worker, had a nice figure to go along with dirty-blonde hair and blue eyes.

Jan and Becky explained that they were from the Toronto area of Canada and had come to Madeira Beach with Jan's mother in mid-May after completing their college final exams. The three women stayed at a condominium owned by Jan's aunt and uncle, who flew down to join them.

On Mother's Day, Sunday, May 14, Jan cooked dinner for her mom and aunt in the condo. After dinner, Jan and Becky headed out to meet some friends at John's Pass, a boat dock area with restaurants and shops, about a fifteen-minute walk from the condo. Around 9:30 p.m. they walked across the street and headed up Gulf Boulevard, the town's main road. They stopped at a 7-Eleven convenience store on their way. Shortly after leaving the store with some beer and snacks, a man called out to them. He was standing by a dark-colored Jeep in the store's parking lot.

The man was "very friendly, very jovial, very gentleman-like," Becky recalled. He walked over to the two young women and asked if they were tourists traveling in the area. When they said they were from Canada, he told them that he lived in Florida, but had resided in upstate New York previously, practically on the Canadian border.

The man introduced himself as Dave Posner. He said he was 33 years old and worked in the roofing business. He was tan with a pot belly, strawberry-blonde hair, and a light-blonde moustache. He came across as personable and good-natured.

They talked about snowfall in Canada compared to upstate New York, but after a few minutes, the two women noticed that they needed to get going.

"It was nice meeting you," Jan told the amicable stranger, "but we need to go meet our friends at John's Pass."

"I'm going that direction if you want a ride," Dave said, flashing a friendly smile. "It wouldn't be any problem at all."

"That's okay, we can walk," Jan replied.

"It's silly for you to have to walk there when I'll be going right by it anyway," Dave insisted good-naturedly. "Come on, let me give you a ride. It won't be any trouble at all, really."

Jan and Becky glanced at each other. They *were* running late and a ride would be a lot faster than walking, so they figured why not. They hopped into Dave's Isuzu Trooper and he seemed happy to have their company. During the five-minute drive, Dave made small talk and brought up that he owned a boat.

"I have a large boat docked about two hours from here," he said. "You two should go on a boat ride with me. We can even fish while we're out."

"Thank you, that's really nice," Becky replied. "We'll definitely keep that in mind."

When they arrived at the John's Pass, Becky went inside one of the restaurants to find their friends, while Jan stayed in the parking lot and continued talking with Dave.

"You know, you're not in a very good area," Dave cautioned. "I've worked around here and it's not a good area. You should really be careful having that beer," he said, indicating the six pack the two women had bought at 7-Eleven. "Just be careful about who you're talking to and watch your purses and jewelry," Dave continued with a look of concern on his face. "This is a high crime area."

He was "very friendly, very warm. He sort of drew you into him in terms of invoking your trust," Jan later recalled. "He seemed very concerned about us."

As they walked toward the pier, Becky went ahead with their friends, while Jan strolled a few steps behind with Dave. His persistence persuaded her. She agreed to an afternoon boat ride the next day. He would pick them up at Don's Dock, a boat service and fuel facility, at mid-afternoon. Becky had been receptive to the idea of a boat ride when Dave first mentioned it, but when Jan told her the plan Becky changed her mind.

"Oh, come on Becky," Jan pleaded, "he's going to be coming a long way and I told him that both of us would go."

But Becky still refused. The next morning, Jan tried again to convince her to go, again to no avail.

"I can't cancel now," Jan said. "I have no way of getting a hold of Dave."

"Why don't you just go," Becky told her. "You go have a good time and I'll be here when you get back."

Seeing that Becky had made up her mind, Jan packed sandwiches and soda for her and Dave and walked down to Don's Dock at the end of the Madeira Beach Boardwalk. When she got to the dock, she saw Dave in his boat, circling the area. She waved and he picked her up at the end of the dock.

"Where's Becky?" he asked as she stepped aboard.

"She decided not to come," Jan replied.

"Why?" Dave frowned.

"She just didn't feel like it, but she might come next time," Jan said apologetically.

"That's too bad," Dave said, "because she's going to miss a really nice day."

She could see his disappointment, but he quickly shrugged it off and steered the boat away, heading out along the shoreline. He "was very nice, friendly, warm" and seemed to enjoy acting as a tour guide and showing her the sights. He showed her how to bait a hook and fish in deep water. He even pulled up a crab trap so she could see how crabs were caught for the local restaurants.

After several hours, the boat lurched a little and Dave frowned.

"We have to go back for a while," he told her. "I have to take care of something with the boat. You can go home and get dinner while I get the engine fixed. And get your camera so we can take pictures of the sunset. Try to get Becky to come too. It'll be fun."

He dropped her back off at the dock at about 6:30 p.m. and told her to meet him there again in an hour since the sun would be setting shortly after 8:00 p.m. When Jan returned to the condo, she tried to talk Becky into coming along for the sunset cruise.

"We've had a really nice time," Jan told her. "We didn't have a chance to do much fishing, but we'll get to do that more tonight. And the sunset is supposed to be really nice on the water. He really wants you to see it and he asked me again to get you. Why don't you come along?"

But Becky still declined, so Jan grabbed her camera and left. When she got back to the dock, Dave was waiting.

"I thought you were going to get Becky to come with us?" he asked, clearly irritated that she was alone.

"I'm sorry," Jan said. "She just doesn't want to come."

The look on Dave's face let her know that he was not happy, but he forced a smile and helped Jan back on board.

"Her loss," he shrugged.

After Jan settled in, Dave steered the boat underneath the John's Pass bridge, eventually stopping and anchoring near Treasure Island. He retrieved some fishing poles and they cast out the lines. They talked and fished for a while before he brought up the anchor, started the engine, and steered further out into the Gulf of Mexico, heading straight toward the setting sun. He let her drive the boat some, standing behind the captain's chair and leaning in close as he showed her how to use the throttle.

After a while, Dave stopped the boat again. The sun began to dip beyond the watery horizon as if it was being swallowed by the sea.

"Why don't I take a picture of you on the bow so you can show your boyfriend," Dave said. After taking her picture, he handed her the camera. "Here, take a picture of me too so you have something to remember me by."

Filling the sky with a brilliant combination of red and orange, the sunset was as spectacular as Dave had promised, and Jan enjoyed every moment of the vivid twilight. But as the last rays of light faded away and darkness began descending, she started getting nervous. The reality dawned on her that she was alone on a boat, at night, miles from shore with a man she barely knew.

"This has been so much fun," she said with a smile to hide her concern, "but I should really be getting back.

Dave ignored her.

"You know, you look really good in that swimsuit," he said. "You're a real nice-looking lady."

"Thank you," Jan replied nervously.

"Why don't you come over here and give me a hug?"

"Thank you for the compliment," Jan said, "but I don't really want to hug you."

If her host heard her, he did not show it.

"Yeah, you're a real nice-looking lady," he said as he continued staring at her.

He leaned over and grabbed her arm, pulling her to him.

"You are going to have sex with me," he growled.

"If you lay one hand on me, I'll charge you with rape," she warned as she stepped away from him and moved to the back of the boat.

He looked at her and laughed.

"You think anybody's going to hear you out here?"

She glanced around desperately. She could still see lights on the distant shore, but they were too far away for anyone to see or hear her. Dave glared at her and grinned.

"You're going to have sex with me," he repeated. "There's no way around it. What are you going to do? Jump out of the boat?"

She screamed as he grabbed her by the wrists and held her hands over her head. He sat back on the passenger seat and pulled his pants down.

"Suck on it," he said.

"No, please," she stammered faintly.

He took the back of her head and pushed her face into his lap. The tightness of his grip told her that she better obey his command. After a little while, he stopped her and put a towel on the floor of the boat. He pushed her down onto the towel and she screamed.

"Shut up! Shut up!" he bellowed. "If you don't shut the fuck up, I'm going to tape your mouth!" he said pointing at a roll of grey duct tape. "Do you want that?"

Her screams quieted to sobs as he pulled her bikini bottom off.

"You're going to have sex with me," he said eagerly. "Is it really worth losing your life over?"

The weight of his words crushed her. She stopped resisting. When he discovered she was menstruating, he pulled her tampon out and tossed it over the side of the boat. Then he rolled her over onto her knees and started trying to penetrate her anally.

"No, no, please don't do that. I have rectal cancer," she lied. "That would hurt really bad, please don't."

Her plea worked. He stopped, but turned her over and had intercourse with her missionary style.

"You have a fucking nice pussy," he said as he slid in and out of her. "You have a really fucking nice pussy."

After he ejaculated, he stopped and pulled his pants back on.

"Now clean yourself up," he said tossing her a thermos with water in it. As she did so, he opened her camera, ripped the film out, and threw it overboard.

"I know you're going to report this," he told her as she huddled shivering in a corner of the boat, "but please give me a chance to go home and tell my little old mother. She'll be really upset if a police officer arrives at the door. It will kill her."

He headed back to shore, occasionally turning on the boat's

spotlight to see channel marker. He eventually let her off on the opposite side of the channel from Don's Dock.

"Watch your step," he said as she stepped gingerly off the boat.

~

Becky became concerned when it started getting dark and Jan had not yet returned, so she went down to the docks at John's Pass to wait for her. After waiting a while, she walked back to the condominium and learned from Jan's mom that Jan had already returned, taken a bath, and gone to bed.

When Becky checked on Jan the next morning, she broke down in tears.

"He raped me," she said.

PART II

"People don't realize that the information they have might be the one piece of the puzzle we need. Their information could put it all together"

– St. Petersburg Police Department Detective JJ Geoghegan

SEVEN

Based on Jan and Becky's description of the rapist, police prepared a composite sketch of "Dan Posner." On November 3, the St. Petersburg Police Department issued a press release of the sketch accompanied by a description of the suspect as a white male, 37 to 40 years old, about 5-foot-9, 190 to 200 pounds, short reddish-blond hair, mustache, and a leathery, tan complexion. The release included a description of the suspect's boat as a 17-foot fiberglass powerboat with a white interior and hull, a blue top, and yellow Volvo engine. The suspect had grey duct tape and an assortment of ropes on the boat. He smoked Marlboro cigarettes and drove a dark blue, 4-door Isuzu Trooper with tinted windows. As a result of the sketch, over 100 phone calls from the public flooded the police department.

Jo Ann Steffey, living at 10713 Dalton Avenue in the

Tampa Shores subdivision, was one of thousands who saw the composite sketch on the news that night. She immediately noticed its resemblance to the man who lived two houses down from her.

"It gave me the willies," she later recalled.

Steffey had seen the man in his yard and driveway several times. She had also seen his boat. It had a white hull and blue top cover. She noticed too that he had the same type of vehicle as the person the police were looking for and his vehicle had a trailer hitch for a boat. After mulling it over in her mind, Steffey went so far as to mention her thoughts about the sketch to family members. However, she decided not to call the police. She could not say for certain that her neighbor was the man in the sketch, and she did not want to falsely accuse someone of such a crime.

"I was told those are serious accusations and I better be sure before I called police," Steffey remembered, thinking back to discussions she had about her initial suspicions.

Even so, she clipped the composite sketch from her newspaper and kept it under a magnet on her refrigerator.

Investigators subsequently learned about a rape involving two young women who had met a white male with reddish-blonde hair in Hudson Beach in April, only a month prior to the Madeira Beach rape. The man acted very friendly and introduced himself as "Mr. Wright," to which one of the women responded, "Not my Mr. Right." The man invited the two women to go for a ride on his blue-and-white boat with a male friend of his. The women accepted, but became afraid when the man drove out into the Gulf of Mexico and said that he wanted to get better acquainted. They managed to convince him that they had friends waiting for them on the beach, and the man eventually took them back.

Of the hundreds of tips called in following release of the composite sketch of the Madeira Beach rapist, many callers thought their husband or ex-boyfriend committed the crimes. One caller reported having a dream in which the killer walked on water and beckoned the women to come to him, causing them to drown. Although none of the calls moved detectives closer to identifying the suspect, they continued examining the registration of every small boat in the state as well as all registrations of black Isuzu Troopers, the car the rapist was believed to be driving.

"It's a long, tedious, time-consuming process of elimination," said Major Cliff Fouts.

Meanwhile, Jan Bradley's rapist, and the Rogers' killer, remained on the loose.

EIGHT

As Hal Rogers prepared for the first Christmas without his family, he decided that rather than spending the holiday in an empty house, he wanted to be where his wife and two daughters had spent some of their last moments.

On a cold and rainy December 23, Hal arrived in Tampa, driving the same Oldsmobile Calais that Joan, Michelle, and Christe had used for their vacation. Record-breaking low temperatures throughout the state seemed to follow him, making it feel more like winter in Ohio than Florida. For the first time anyone could remember, snow flurries fell from the sky in the Tampa Bay area, part of the far edge of the largest snowstorm in history in the Southeast.

Hal drove to the ramp where his wife and daughters had boarded their killer's boat. He stood at the edge of the water and looked out toward the horizon, trying to imagine how his family had felt as a stranger ferried them from the water's edge, taking them from the safety of shore, far away out into the bay.

NINE

The record frigid temperatures continued through Christmas and lingered until the massive cold front retreated north just before the new year. Unlike the warming weather, the Rogers case remained cold, but events were unfolding that would ensure the investigation did not remain dormant much longer.

Late one Saturday night, Jo Ann Steffey took a break from studying for one of her college courses and walked into the kitchen, passing by the police sketch of the Madeira Beach rapist that was still secured under magnets on her refrigerator. By the kitchen counter, she glanced outside the window and froze. Her neighbor, the man who so closely resembled the composite sketch, was standing next to her driveway underneath a streetlight, staring at her house.

Steffey quickly stepped back from the window, turned off

the kitchen light, and peered outside again. She could still see the man looking toward the house and the thought that he had seen her sent chills up Steffey's spine. Finally, after what seemed forever, he turned his head away and appeared to call out to someone. Then a small dog bounded over to him and he turned and walked away.

∼

On June 2, 1990, to mark the one-year anniversary of the murders of Joan, Michelle, and Christe Rogers, bells tolled simultaneously at six churches across Van Wert County. Days earlier at Crestview High School's graduation ceremony in the school's small gym in Convoy, Ohio, an empty chair sat vacant among 58 other chairs occupied by graduating seniors. The empty chair had a single rose on its seat in memory of their missing classmate, Michelle.

∼

By the end of the first year of the Rogers investigation over 1200 leads had been followed with detectives no closer to catching the killer. While not officially declared a cold case, senior police officials realized that the Rogers investigation was essentially stalled so they decided to shake things up. After reviewing the status of the case, the head of the St. Petersburg Police Department's Detective Division formed the Major Crimes Squad, allocating several personnel to the newly formed task force, including Detective Glen Moore. Recently transferred to homicide in November 1989, Moore was a senior detective with over twenty years of law enforcement experience in patrol, vice and narcotics, and burglaries. Other law enforcement personnel joining the new task force included Florida Department of Law Enforcement Special Agent John Halliday and FBI Special Agent James Ramey, recognized as an expert in psychological profiling.

A former football player who married his high school sweetheart, Detective Moore had earned the nickname "Boomer" twenty years earlier during his rookie year on the force due to his strength and athleticism. Now Moore oversaw a handpicked group of St. Petersburg Police Department detectives that included Cindra Cummings and John (J.J.) Geoghegan. Although nearly forty detectives had worked various aspects of the Rogers case in the early stages of the investigation, the Major Crimes Squad would investigate the case using a focused team effort.

During his review of the case file, Detective Moore came across a Xerox copy of the Clearwater Beach brochure that had been found in Joan Rogers's car at the Courtney Campbell Causeway boat ramp. The brochure had handwriting on it that appeared to be directions to the Days Inn on Rocky Point. Moore was surprised to learn that the brochure's handwriting had not previously been explored, whether inadvertently or due to a decision to focus on other evidence and leads.

Noting references on the brochure to Boy Scout Boulevard and Columbus, Moore determined to focus on the area of Dale

Mabry Highway where the two roads came together. He believed that a handwritten "X" on the brochure corresponded to an area between that intersection and Interstate 275 encompassing several blocks of commercial businesses. With the new focus of the investigation, detectives spent nearly a week canvassing the area and interviewing business owners around the location.

Detective Moore often returned to the Days Inn motel at Rocky Point to try to retrace the Rogers' steps to see if there was anything else that he had missed about the case.

"I put myself in Hal Rogers's shoes," Moore said. "What was he feeling like? How could I let that go? If this was my wife and my daughters, I would search until the end of the earth to find out who did it."

Moore also started studying other serial killers to get a sense of how their minds worked. He wanted to better understand the darker side of human nature, hoping that getting inside the mind of a murderer would give him insight into who could have committed the Rogers triple murder.

A deeply religious man, Moore believed that murderer personified the expanding power of evil in the modern world.

"I was out to catch a demon," Detective Moore said.

Whatever demonic force controlled the Rogers' killer, and whoever the killer turned out to be, Moore prayed for God's guidance and assistance in bringing him to justice.

TEN

In the Fall of 1990, Detective Moore traveled across the Atlantic for a week-long stay in England. He was eager to learn about HOLMES (Home Office Large Major Enquiry System), a sophisticated computer system developed by Scotland Yard, London's renowned police force, for investigating major criminal cases. Tasked with organizing information in massive, complex investigations, HOLMES had been developed in 1984 by British investigators frustrated by the Yorkshire Ripper case in which Peter Sutcliffe murdered at least 13 women in northern England in the 1970s. Lauded for its ability to sift through "mountains of information at a rate of more than 1-million words a minute," HOLMES made its debut by helping investigate the terrorist bombing of a Pan Am 747 jumbo jet over Lockerbie, Scotland, which killed 259 people on board and 11 people on the ground on December 21, 1988.

In December 1990, the Rogers case became the first criminal investigation in the United States to utilize HOLMES. With Moore newly trained on how to use the computer system, the St. Petersburg Police Department put HOLMES to work in the Rogers case, hopeful that the $500,000 system (equivalent to approximately $1,066,500 in 2022) would prove to be as successful a sleuth as its famous fictitious namesake.

On the morning of January 27, 1991, Detectives Geoghegan and Cummings, along with FBI Special Agent Ramey, flew from Tampa International Airport to Van Wert, Ohio. They arrived around 3:00 p.m., then drove about 15 miles to the Rogers farm in Wilshire. The three investigators spent nearly three hours talking to Hal in his home, covering topics that included where he was when his wife and daughters traveled to Florida and whether he knew of anyone who might have wanted to harm them. The three investigators noted that Hal seemed "very cooperative and composed" throughout the questioning. Alone on his farm, Hal Rogers was "just trying to survive" and get through each day the best he could. He dealt with the grief one day at a time, hour by hour, minute by minute.

For the next nine days, Geoghegan, Cummings, and Ramey worked from early morning until midnight interviewing well over fifty witnesses. They even interviewed Hal Rogers again, this time at the Van Wert Sheriff's Office, before returning to Tampa on February 5. Many of the witnesses told the investigators that the Rogers women were "very friendly" and probably would have accepted an invitation to go on a boat ride if offered.

About a week after Detective Geoghegan returned from Ohio, he received a tip from Hillsborough County Jail inmate Joseph Hair that a man named Gregory Ross had committed the Rogers triple homicide. In his early to mid-20's, the 6-foot-2, two-hundred-pound Ross owned a white and blue colored Cobia boat with two large outboard motors and a 1989 dark blue or black colored Ford Bronco.

Hair described Ross as a construction worker who was "very neat and meticulous with his vehicle, clothes, and boat." He was "into bondage and S & M, Satanism, masochism, liked to tie people up, and also liked to be tied up." Ross liked hard rock music, especially AC/DC, and had a particular attraction for teenaged girls.

When Ross took Hari fishing around the Gandy Bridge, Ross showed him pubic hairs he claimed came from the Rogers women and he said that he was going to make a new fishing fly out of it. He also told Hair that "there used to be shark bait out here [in the water], but that the police had already found it," a reference that Hair took as meaning the Rogers' bodies. Ross purportedly bragged that he "dumped the old fish first, then the other two fish were very obliging," and that he and his buddies had "filled every hole before we dumped them." Ross also said that he "liked poking the youngest fish of the three" and call her an "awesome fuck." Ross claimed to have met the three Rogers women while on lunch break one day. He helped them with a loose wire in their car and they asked him where the beaches were.

Like previous leads, Hair's tip seemed promising at first, but despite contacting virtually every sheriff's department in the state, Detective Geoghegan was not able to locate Gregory Ross. Hair later admitted that he made up the story about Ross in an attempt to get his step-father, Charles Hair, out of jail. Geoghegan concluded that Joseph Hair likely obtained information about the Rogers case from the news media and then used it to make up his story about Ross.

~

As HOLMES sifted through reams of new information about the case, Geoghegan learned from Steve Porter, a Pinellas County Attorney's Office investigator, that the Pinellas Park Police Department was working a homicide that had some similarities to the Rogers triple murder. Porter told Geoghegan that the Pinellas Park case "may possibly be related to the Madeira Beach rape case, which may also be related to the Rogers homicide."

After meeting with a counterpart at the Pinellas Park Police Department, Geoghegan concluded that although there were "indeed some similarities" between the two cases, the "other facts of the cases and the lifestyles of the victims in both cases were totally different." The Pinellas Park suspect was a known drug smuggler who owned a 45-foot boat and liked "strange and kinky sex, including bondage," but he developed a cocaine habit and had been "going down-hill since.' In ruling out the suspect as the Rogers' killer, Geoghegan also decided it was extremely unlikely that the Rogers women would have struck up a conversation with him, let alone agree to go out on his boat. Geoghegan noted that they likely would have avoided him because he was "very rough and tattered looking" and "does not have an appearance which would convey a feeling of security or acceptability to a friendly chat from a stranger."

Investigators also reviewed the lead about a dark colored Bronco or Blazer seen in the Days Inn Rocky Point parking lot on the day that the three Rogers women checked into the motel. They used HOLMES to analyze records provided by the Ford Motor Company detailing all sales of dark colored Broncos throughout the United States during the three years prior to the murders. HOLMES also ran a similar analysis of General Motors records regarding dark colored Blazer purchases.

Another new lead came from an anonymous caller who insisted that Donald Miller, 32, and his brother Leslie Miller, 30, had something to do with the Rogers triple homicide. Detective Geoghegan learned that Donald was currently serving time for lewd and lascivious acts on an 11-year-old girl, who he was babysitting when the acts occurred. The girl was the niece of Donald's girlfriend at the time. A Temple Terrace police officer when the acts occurred, Donald had been rejected by the Tampa Police Department after he displayed a "cocky and negative" attitude during his employment interview, which included him using foul and derogatory language such as calling his ex-wife a bitch and making racial slurs. The interviewing officer had written in his evaluation in large bold letters: "VERY POOR CANDIDATE WITH OBVIOUS PREJUDICE AND ATTITUDE PROBLEMS." Yet, in his personnel file from the Temple Terrace Police Department, Donald's supervising officer recorded that he was "one of the best uniform officers that Temple Terrace has," and he had won Officer of the Year there in 1989. Despite Donald Miller's accolades, Geoghegan considered him to be a legitimate suspect in the Rogers case.

On April 3, 1991, Geoghegan, Cummings, and Moore met with members of the FBI's Behavioral Sciences Unit (BSU) in Quantico, VA, in hopes of producing a psychological profile of the Rogers' killer. The BSU started profiling criminals during the 1970s by using specific crime scene information. Its methods had proven so successful that local law enforcement authorities began requesting the unit's assistance and eventually BSU began helping agencies nationwide on select cases. Sexual homicide cases made up a large portion of the cases in which BSU agreed to lend a hand, largely because of the immense public pressure law enforcement felt from the widespread publicity and fear such cases often generated. Those cases also tended to be the most difficult to solve due to the random and apparently motiveless nature of the majority of sexual homicides.

The following month, a production crew from the popular TV show, *Unsolved Mysteries*, filmed in the Tampa Bay area to recreate the Rogers murders. While in town to serve as an advisor for the episode, Hal Rogers took a lie detector test and easily passed, putting an end to suspicions about his involvement in the crimes once and for all.

Everything Moore and the Rogers Task Force now knew about the murders led them to conclude that the killer was someone from the local area. After committing the triple homicide, he had simply blended back into the community, concealed again as an anonymous member of the public.

ELEVEN

Heeding a recommendation by the FBI to use the news media to generate leads, Detective Moore called a news conference on May 20 and released a partial profile of the Rogers' killer. Standing in front of a blown-up image of the Rogers' trip itinerary, Moore announced that Joan, Michelle, and Christe were victims of a "thrill killer" who acted out a fantasy by sexually assaulting the women and enjoying their fear as they were thrown into the bay while still alive.

Moore cited the profile's prediction that the offender "receives his gratification from the control of and domination over the victims," and "derives pleasure and satisfaction from their suffering." Although he had gagged his three victims with duct tape, he did not blindfold them or cover their eyes with tape because he "wanted to see their terror." He did not commit the rapes for sexual pleasure. Rather, it was exercising power over other human beings in a violent manner – subjugating them through acts of violence and dominating them physically and psychologically – that drove him to commit his crimes.

The killer had been planning a way to fulfill his fantasies, and Joan, Michelle, and Christe's friendly personalities had made them "easy prey." Characteristics of the crime indicated that the killer was an "organized" murderer, meaning that

(1) the offense was planned,

(2) the victims were likely strangers,

(3) the killer controlled the conversation, using a ruse to gain the victims' trust,

(4) he exercised control during the crime itself,

(5) restraints were used to render his victims subdued and submissive so that he could exert his control freely,

(6) he committed sexual assaults prior to killing the victims,

(7) he transported the victims to an area where they would be helpless, and

(8) he disposed of the bodies to try to conceal the crime.

"This is a very heinous crime, particularly when you have family members probably seeing each other being violated sexually and then seeing your mother, sister, or daughter thrown into the water to die a horrible death," Moore told the reporters in attendance.

Then he looked into the news cameras as if he wanted to

speak directly to the monster who committed the heinous crimes.

"I would say the honeymoon is over for this killer. We're going to hunt him down until we find him."

Having considered the FBI's input, Moore's team now believed that two people participated in the crimes because there were no bruises or defense wounds on the three women's bodies, indicating that they were easily controlled by the perpetrators. The dominant of the two would mostly likely be a neat and meticulous person, very controlled and confident, with social skills that enabled him to come across as non-threatening.

In Detective Moore's mind, one of the most important aspects of the FBI profile was its indication that the suspect would be the "guy next door." He would not stand out or blatantly appear as "some monster."

"This will be a normal person who goes to work every day," Moore explained to the reporters attending. "He could be somebody no one would ever suspect, such as a "relative, a husband, maybe a boyfriend."

Based on his ability to maneuver a boat in Tampa Bay after dark and the familiarity with the bay waters that such navigating required, the killer was likely a resident of the area. The recovery of the Rogers' bodies probably surprised him because he thought that the concrete blocks would keep them submerged. It was also likely that he displayed an avid interest in the case that could include clipping newspaper articles about it.

The FBI profile predicted that he would have killed prior to the Rogers murders. It would be extremely unusual for someone to kill three people at once without having "practiced" by killing a single victim on one or more prior occasions. Homicidal criminals typically worked their way up from one crime to another, gaining confidence, becoming bolder, and being willing to take more risks as they progressed in experience.

Sexual homicides often begin as fantasies in the offender's mind which provide a way to escape from what he perceives to be an unjust reality. The fantasy fulfills the offender's need for control and sense of entitlement, becoming a "private and powerful reality" in his mind. Over time, the perpetrator feels compelled to make the fantasy into reality, and after successfully enacting it the offender relives the crime in his mind to learn how to better enact the fantasy. As the killer gains experience and learns from each crime, aspects of the crimes become routine and he needs more and more excitement to achieve satisfaction, eventually becoming sadistic if he was not already that way to begin with.

The FBI now believed that the Rogers murders were the work of a serial killer. The prospect of a serial killer on the loose put more pressure on the task force to find him since it was almost a certainty that he would keep on killing unless stopped.

TWELVE

At the end of May, stalks of corn and soybeans began sprouting up through the fertile soil of family farms dotting the twisting, narrow roads of western Ohio. Nearly two years removed from the Rogers triple homicide, residents of Willshire, Ohio continued to struggle with the psychological impact of the crime. In their case file, investigators noted that the murders "have totally devastated everyone in the victims' home town and the loss of their lives will have lifelong effects on all who knew them." Of course, no one had been impacted more than Hal Rogers.

"It's been really hard on Hal," said Frank Evans, a local farmer and family friend. "He's never gotten over it. He still wonders why it happened, why they had to die. Something like that can shake your faith. It's shaken the whole town's faith."

Police increased the $5,000 reward for information leading

to the capture of the Rogers' killer to $25,000 in hopes of enticing the anonymous caller who provided information about the Miller brothers to call again.

"We've been able to verify a lot of the information and we feel very good about this information," explained Sgt. Moore. "In order for us to go further in this investigation, we need to talk to the caller again. This is by far the best thing we've had yet."

Detective Cummings, an experienced rock climber with some expertise in tying ropes and knots, analyzed the knots used on the ropes that had bound the Rogers family. Cummings concluded that all of the knots for the women's hands had been tied in the same hurried manner and that the same person had tied them for all three women. The knots for their feet appeared to have been more carefully tied. Cummings's findings supported the new theory that a lone killer threatened the three women at gunpoint and quickly secured their hands. Once their hands had been tied, he could then take more time in securing their feet. The scenario also explained how one of them managed to free her hand: those knots simply had not been tied securely in the killer's haste to subdue all three women. The position of the rope knots on the bodies suggested that both Michelle and Christe had struggled to free themselves, leading Cummings to conclude that they had been thrown into the water while still alive.

Hal Rogers shared that belief.

"I know in my own heart that they were thrown in alive. I know that. I can just feel it," said Hal.

Death by drowning is not a pleasant way to die. The instinct to breathe is strong, but the instinct to not breathe underwater is nearly as strong and a drowning person will not inhale until she is on the verge of unconsciousness. At that point, so much carbon dioxide has built up in the person's blood that chemical sensors in the brain trigger an involuntary breath, an unpleasant process that pulls water into the mouth and windpipe, flooding the lungs. Although the time it takes for this to happen varies depending on age, health, lung capacity, water temperature, and other factors, it takes 87 seconds on average: about 1 ½ minutes of terror-filled torture. As water fills the lungs it passes into the bloodstream and causes electrolyte imbalance and oxygen deprivation, which in turn forces the heart into ventricular fibrillation. Death soon follows.

One person who survived nearly drowning described it this way:

> First there's the fear; the pressing down of lungs that suddenly need to breathe more than ever before. You can't see, you can't breathe, you don't know which way is up or down. Then there's the knowledge that you're about to die. Your lungs burn and your chest feels like it's being compressed right in the center by a giant fist, and pulled apart at the same time... Your ears are throbbing, you can hear your own heartbeat, your own last few pulses. Your limbs feel dead, heavy, and you have no control over them. Your vision goes black eventually, but there are little flashes of sparks as your eyes move, trying to find light.

It would have been virtually impossible for the Rogers women to find any light as they struggled to survive that terrible summer night. Out in the middle of Tampa Bay, the lights from the distant shore might as well have been a million miles away. When they were thrown overboard into the bay to drown, Joan, Michelle, and Christe were engulfed by water as ominously black as it was unforgivably deep.

~

In October, police released a picture of the worn, blue-colored Clearwater Beach brochure containing the misspelled directions "Courtney Cambell Causeway RT 60 Days Inn" handwritten on the back. Detective Moore explained that his team of detectives tried "every way possible on our own to figure this out," including by driving the route noted on the brochure in hopes of learning something about what the Rogers women were thinking during their trip. They followed the route from Orlando to Tampa and were able to match the travel time exactly, as well as coming within two-tenths of a mile of matching the mileage on the Rogers' car.

Moore's team believed that the Rogers got lost trying to get to Busch Gardens by exiting I-4 onto Hillsborough Avenue and then missing a small sign that directed motorists to the theme park. Continuing on Hillsborough past the turn off, the women would have come to Dale Mabry Highway where they turned south. They then likely realized they were lost and stopped someplace south of Columbus Drive to ask for directions.

Another plausible scenario had them driving south on I-275 in Tampa and accidentally exiting onto Dale Mabry by inadvertently staying in the far right-hand lane. That part of the interstate did not give much warning before the lane became an exit, and having incorrectly exited, they could have pulled into the parking lot of a McDonalds located just off the interstate, a familiar place to ask for directions and grab lunch. While there, detectives theorized, they met the man who gave them directions to the Days Inn.

Investigators hoped that whoever wrote the directions for them on the brochure might be able to reveal something about the Rogers' plans for the rest of that fateful day.

"Persons they met in Tampa are very important to tell us where the victims were. Maybe during the conversation they would have told them what their plans were for the day," Moore said. "Whatever they can tell us, we need to talk to them."

THIRTEEN

On November 3, 1991, the *Unsolved Mysteries* episode about the Rogers family aired nationwide on NBC during primetime. After the show's broadcast, police received hundreds of tips from viewers, but none of them became substantive leads. However, shortly afterward, Detective Geoghegan spoke to the Metro Dade Police Department about a homicide in Dade County involving a female who was found floating in Biscayne Bay tied with duct tape. Metro Dade detectives advised that the victim was Bridgett Gibbs, sister of Miami Police Captain Arnold Gibbs. She and her boyfriend had been abducted during a robbery, tied with duct tape around both hands, feet, and mouth, and then thrown off a bridge in Biscayne Bay. Despite some similarities, Geoghegan determined that the case was not related to the Rogers homicides. It was simply another lead detectives followed to a dead end, another instance of hope ending in frustration and disappointment.

A police report detailing the investigation conveyed the emotional effects that detectives working the case were experiencing:

> *Homicide investigators, who are normally hardened by the emotional aspects of such cases, have been struck by the unusually cruel nature of this crime. The end result has been an even greater determination to solve the case.*

For Detective Cummings and the others immersed in the investigation the Rogers case had come to feel personal.

"There are things I know about Michelle and Christe that I probably don't know about my own son," she revealed. "We have their pictures on the wall in the office – little girl pictures in front of the Christmas tree. That's what it's all about."

Despite another promising lead not panning out, Cummings continued to hold onto her hope that they would catch the killer.

"I have interview him a hundred times at least in my mind," she said. "I've thought about what I'd say to him."

Six months after it first aired, NBC rebroadcast the *Unsolved Mysteries* episode featuring the Rogers case. Over the next few days, hundreds of new tips were called in to the St. Petersburg Police Department. The tips came from Florida, the Midwest, and up and down the East Coast. One of the callers, Lead No. 1,507, was a woman who said that her sister lived two doors down from a man in Tampa who her sister thought might be the suspect. A detective called the sister and left a message for her, but she never returned the call.

~

On May 13, 1992, as the third anniversary of the Roger murders loomed with police no closer to cracking the case, Detectives Jim Culverson and Mark Deasaro suggested that Joan, Michelle, and Christe's faces be featured on some roadway billboards in an effort to kickstart the case. Detective Moore liked the idea, especially since Patrick Advertising, the company that owned the billboards, agreed to let the police use them – ten in total – without the usual $600 rental charge. Even better, Detective Culverson's dad donated the $1,000 needed to cover the printing costs for what would appear on the billboards.

The billboards carried the heading "WHO KILLED THE ROGERS FAMILY?" in six-foot tall letters above extra-large photos of Joan, Michelle, and Christe, and also featured the offer of a $25,000 reward for information leading to an arrest. One of the billboards went up on North Dale Mabry, the area where police believed Joan, Michelle, and Christe had met their wolf-in-sheep's-clothing killer, the seemingly good Samaritan who had helped them when they were lost.

It was likely that nearly everyone they encountered on their Florida vacation had been friendly and welcoming. Their days at Disney World and other tourist attractions would have reinforced that perspective. When a stranger they had just met gave them directions and then offered to take them on a sunset cruise, they probably did not give it a second thought. Such kindness would have seemed normal at that point. The killer would have been just another friendly face in the Sunshine State. They had no reason to think otherwise.

Since the three women were seen in the Days Inn restaurant around 7:30 p.m., and an expert concluded that the photograph showing the view from their balcony was taken sometime between 6:30 and 8:30 p.m., investigators believed they had boarded the killer's boat between 8:30 and 9:00 p.m. and were murdered after midnight.

"This is probably something he has fantasized about for quite some time and these women just happened along at the wrong time to fulfill his fantasy," Detective Moore stated, reiterating one of the attributes the FBI's psychological profile ascribed to the killer.

After receiving 75 phone calls from members of the public in response to the billboards erected the day before, Moore appeared before reporters again on May 14 to appeal for the public's help. This time he focused on the handwritten directions on the Clearwater Beach tourist brochure, releasing photos of it in the hope that someone would recognize the handwriting.

Police also revealed that a handwriting expert who examined the brochure opined that the man who wrote it was already in a "homicidal mood" when he encountered the Rogers women. The handwriting analyst pointed to the downhill slope of the writing – a "homicidal dip" to the right often found in the writing of people considering suicide or homicide – as well as a line drawn under the directions, to support his conclusion.

There were other unique characteristics of the handwriting as well. The letter "T" was capitalized in the middle of the word "Courtney," while the letter "y" was written four times in the directions. Unlike the "T," the "y" letters were all written differently, something Teresa Stubbs, the FDLE's forensic document expert had never seen before.

"We are saying this is the suspect folks – find the guy," Detective Moore implored, pointing to a blow up of the directions.

Moore's statement to reporters marked a shift from his previous position that police wanted to speak to whoever wrote the directions simply to learn what plans the Rogers women had for the rest of their day.

"This handwriting is the killer's handwriting," he declared. "If we find the writer, we find the killer."

FOURTEEN

Reading through her morning newspaper, Jo Ann Steffey came across a new article about the Rogers case that included a photograph of the handwritten directions from the Clearwater Beach brochure. The more Steffey looked at the handwriting, the more familiar it looked. With her suspicions about the man living two doors down from her still in mind due to his resemblance to the composite sketch of the Madeira Beach rape suspect, Steffey walked next door to see what her friend, Mozelle Smith, thought about the handwriting.

Smith recollected that, two years earlier, the man had built a screened-in addition to one of the rental homes that she owned. After searching through her records, Smith found a work agreement the neighbor had written for her to build the screened enclosure. The $2,776 estimate had been filled out by him on a form "Agreement" with his business letterhead assuring that he was "Licensed-Bonded-Insured." When Steffey and Smith compared them, the man's handwriting on the work agreement matched the handwriting on the Clearwater Beach brochure.

"When we compared the handwriting, my skin crawled," Steffey recalled. "I had never felt a sensation like that before in my life."

"Oh, it was the same all right," Smith agreed. "We knew it right then."

Smith remembered the neighbor as being very personable when she hired him to do the screen work.

"He looked like a tennis player and he was a real charmer," she recalled.

The man's name was Oba Chandler.

Steffey made up her mind. Her initial misgivings about calling the police fell away. In addition to the close handwriting resemblance, there were too many similarities between the man in the composite sketch and the man who lived two houses away from her, and the description released by the police was eerily close to that of her neighbor, the man who introduced himself as "Obie."

"There was something about him that made me uneasy," Steffey said, although she could not point to one thing to explain it. "The hair on the back of my neck stood up the first time I met him," she recalled. "And I'd never had that happen before or since. Maybe he was too friendly. Maybe it was the way he looked at you – he never would look you in the eye."

Civilian investigator Eileen Przybysz answered the phone

when Steffey called the St. Petersburg Police Department. Steffey told her about Chandler's close resemblance to the police sketch and the handwriting match. She also told Przybysz that Chandler owned a boat like that of the suspect and drove a similar car. After Steffey called and spoke to the police, Smith faxed the work estimate to them along with a check that Chandler had endorsed so they could undertake their own comparison of the handwriting.

As the mother of two daughters, Steffey had been deeply impacted by the Rogers murders. She shuddered at imagining her girls meeting the same fate as Michelle and Christe Roges.

"To me, those girls weren't just strangers in a picture," she said grimly. "He had to be stopped."

FIFTEEN

July 30, 1992 proved to be one of the most important days in the three-year-old investigation. Long-time Pinellas County Commissioner Barbara Sheen Todd had followed the Rogers case since the very beginning. As the mother of two girls close in age to Michelle and Christe Rogers, Commissioner Todd took the triple murder personally. She had taken a vested interest in crimes against children since a man exposed himself to one of her daughters at a bus stop, an act that spurred her to help establish the Child Safety Task Force of Tampa Bay.

During breakfast with her husband, an idea popped into Todd's head. Police had already displayed Joan, Michelle, and Christe's photographs on billboards around the Tampa Bay area, so why not do the same thing with the handwritten directions from the Clearwater Beach brochure? That would put the handwriting in view of thousands of motorists, ensuring it would be seen by more people than simply putting a photo of it in the newspaper or on the local news. At her husband's urging, Todd called the St. Petersburg Police Department and she soon had Detective Moore on the line.

At Commissioner Todd's personal request, Patrick Media agreed to donate more billboard space to feature blown-up images of the handwriting on the Clearwater Beach brochure. Appearing beside the handwriting on the billboards was the large bold text: "WHO WROTE THESE DIRECTIONS? You may know who killed the Rogers Family." The billboards also included a reminder about the $25,000 reward being offered and the phone number for the direct line to the detectives working the Rogers case. Although initially reluctant to approve them, Detective Moore called the billboards a "last hurrah" for the 14-member Rogers task force.

On July 30, Moore announced the erection of the boards at a news conference held at Himes Avenue and Columbus Drive near the area of Dale Mabry where the investigative team believed the Rogers had encountered their killer. Commissioner Todd stood beside him, along with Wayne Mack, owner of Patrick Media.

"Normally, our policy is not to discuss evidence or have the public view evidence in unsolved homicide cases," Detective Moore acknowledged. "However, the Rogers case is so unique, and the necessity to capture the killer so compelling, the need to display this evidence overrides normal procedures. We need to locate the writer of this printing," Moore asserted as he pointed to the handwriting. "He will be the killer."

Having seen the announcement of the new billboards, Mozelle Smith's daughter, Dale Curtis, called the St. Petersburg Police Department the very next day. She wanted to know the status of the sample of Oba Chandler's handwriting that her mother and Jo Ann Steffey had provided two months earlier. Unable to find any reference to the Chandler handwriting sample, the person answering the hotline asked Curtis to re-send it. Task force members later determined that the fax Smith and Steffey previously sent was hard to read, and it had been placed in a stack of other leads and essentially forgotten.

Along with the same handwriting sample sent before, Curtis faxed a cover letter reaffirming that *many of us are convinced that this handwriting is the same as the one published in the papers.* She advised that Smith and Steffey had considered getting their own handwriting expert to analyze the sample, but *due to Commissioner Todd's new personal interest we have recontacted you.* This time the sample did not fall through the cracks.

Detective Geoghegan met with Mozelle Smith at her house a few days later to get the originals of a check endorsed by Chandler and the work agreement that she previously faxed to the police. After comparing the handwriting on the samples to the handwriting on the Clearwater Beach brochure, Geoghegan reached the same conclusion as Steffey and Smith.

"You didn't have to be a handwriting expert to see it," Geoghegan said. "I knew at that point we had a 50-50 chance. He either killed them or gave them directions."

Task force members quickly noticed that a photograph of

Oba Chandler obtained from probation officials looked just like the composite sketch of the Madeira Beach rape suspect. To keep Chandler from getting wind of their suspicions, the task force came up with a code name to use instead of his real name. They called him the "Tin Man," evoking the character from *The Wizard of Oz* who had the machine-metal body and lacked a human heart.

Detective Geoghegan learned that Chandler owned the 10709 Dalton Avenue house beginning in 1988, but the mortgage lender had foreclosed on the property in October 1991. As he and other investigators dug deeper into Chandler's past, they continued efforts to determine his current whereabouts. Believing him to be living on the east coast of Florida near Daytona Beach, they discovered that he had an extensive criminal record:

1968 – Arrested for defrauding an innkeeper in
Cincinnati, OH
1969 – Arrested for petty larceny in Cincinnati
1969 – Arrested for concealing stolen goods in
Cincinnati consisting of 21 stolen wigs and a stolen
television. Sentenced to one to seven years in Ohio State
Reformatory. Transferred to Lebanon Correctional
Institute in May 1969.
1970 – Paroled
1970 – Arrested for speeding and driving without a
license in Cincinnati
1971 – Arrested for disorderly conduct in Cincinnati

1971 – Arrested for larceny in Cincinnati

1972 – Arrested for breaking and entering in Cincinnati

1973 – Arrested for prowling in Cincinnati

1973 – Bond forfeited and warrant issued for his arrest.

1975 – Arrested on charge of fugitive from justice in Orlando, FL. Placed on one year probation.

1976 – Warrant issued for arrest for violating probation

1976 – Arrested for burglary, armed robbery, and kidnapping in Volusia County.

1977 – Jan: Sentenced to 10 years for robbery; nolle pross entered on other charges. May: Escaped from prison work detail at Doctor Inlet at Jacksonville. Assumed name of James Thomas Wright.

1978 – Arrested in Altamonte Springs for loitering and prowling (used name James Wright).

1979 – Arrested in Orlando for loitering and prowling (used name James Wright).

1981 – Arrested in Orlando for petty theft for breaking into a soft drink machine (used name James Wright).

1984 – Arrested in Tampa on warrant for 1977 prison escape

1984-86 – Served time in Union Correctional Institute

1987 – Released in the Duval County/Jacksonville area

During his two decades of run-ins with law enforcement, Chandler had used the names Oba Chandler, James Wright, and Oba Leiby, and at various times claimed employment as an x-ray technician from Orlando, an aluminum contractor from Daytona Beach, a retiree from Tampa, an unemployed apartment manager from New York, and a mechanical draftsman from Cincinnati. He frequently moved around the state, residing in Jacksonville, Land O'Lakes, Tarpon Springs, Tampa, Odessa, and Sunrise over a five-year period from 1986 to 1991.

In October 1991, he and his wife moved into a house on DeLeon Drive in a middle-class subdivision called "The Woods" in the city of Port Orange located a little south of Daytona Beach.

Counting his current wife, Debra, Chandler had married four times and fathered seven children:

Dec 1964 – Married to Kathleen Louks (Kentucky). Divorced Aug 1965.
Dec 1966 – Married to Diane Southward (North Carolina). Divorced Dec 1967.
Feb 1969 – Married to Jennifer Jones, a bunny at the Playboy Club in Cincinnati, Ohio. Divorced 1972.
May 1988 – Married Debra Whiteman (Florida).

In a bizarre twist, Chandler had worked as a confidential informant for the United States Customs Agency in 1991. In July of that year, he advised Customs officers that Steve Segura, a St. Petersburg maintenance supervisor, wanted to buy marijuana. Chandler set up the buy in the West Shore Mall parking lot and Segura was arrested along with Chandler's nephew-in-law, who Chandler had used to set up the buy. Having the alleged perpetrator of a heinous triple homicide working as a confidential informant for a federal agency became yet another bizarre twist to the story.

After Chandler's arrest for the Madeira Beach rape, Segura saw his picture in a newspaper article and called the newspaper to comment about the story. Whether driven by a desire for revenge or simply motivated to share a truthful observation, Segura had nothing positive to say about Chandler.

"The first time I saw Obie I thought he was a little weird," Segura recalled. "He was a little sicko. You can tell a sicko by the twinkle in their eye."

Results of a fingerprint analysis showed that Chandler's fingerprints did not match prints found on the Clearwater Beach brochure. However, a palm print found on the brochure clearly matched Chandler's right palm print.

On September 9, Detective Geoghegan and a Marine Officer met at Chandler's former house on Dalton Ave to determine how long it would have taken him to travel by boat to Don's Dock in Madeira Beach. Moving at an average speed of 30-32 mph, the trip took them 1 hour, 45 minutes, and the total distance came to 41.3 miles. They followed the canal that ran behind Chandler's residence to a larger canal known as Channel A, running north and south along the west side of Tampa Shores Subdivision. Continuing down Channel A led them to Upper Old Tampa Bay, a large body of water north of the Courtney Campbell Causeway Bridge. They went south under the Causeway Bridge, under the Howard Franklin

Bridge, and then under the Gandy Bridge, before following the main ship channel southwest toward the Sunshine Skyway Bridge. Passing under two draw bridges they entered the Intercoastal Waterway and proceeded north to Don's Dock at the John's Pass area in Madeira Beach.

The next day, over 1700 miles away in Hamilton, Ontario, both Jan Bradley and Becky Mathews picked Chandler's photograph out of a six-photo lineup. When Jan saw Chandler's photo a "feeling of horror" went through her mind as she flashed back to the May 1989 night on her rapist's boat.

"Do you mind if I turn his photograph over?" she asked. "It's really bothering me."

~

While police gathered evidence to strengthen their case against Chandler, he was busy committing new crimes. Around 9:45 p.m. on September 11, Chandler robbed two sales representatives of Van-Lightner, a wholesale jewelry manufacturing company, after they got out of their rental car in the parking lot of the Pinellas Park Residence Inn where they were staying for a jewelry show.

"Leave your purse and wallet! Don't look at me! Keep your face down!" he yelled while pointing a large handgun at them and speeding away in their car with $750,000 worth of jewelry in the trunk.

A little too late to help the Van-Lightner jewelers, the task force began 24-hour surveillance of Oba Chandler's house, following him wherever he went, careful to rotate the units tailing him so that he did not become suspicious. Police also seized *Gypsy I*, the 1976, 21-foot Bayliner boat previously owned by Chandler, and stored it securely on their impound lot. This seemingly routine act would prove to be of immense, albeit unanticipated, importance in the future.

SIXTEEN

With the addition of Jan Bradley's photo lineup identification, Detective Moore's group decided they had enough evidence to warrant arresting Oba Chandler. But only hours before they planned to make the arrest, Chandler walked out of his house and drove away in a blue Toyota Corolla. Police tails in unmarked cars followed him north up I-75. To keep Chandler from noticing the cars following him, they fell back at various intervals and let a surveillance plane take over for periods of time. The cars had instructions to stop him before he crossed the state line, but he exited the interstate at Lake City, Florida, as a thunderstorm approached the area.

The surveillance plane was watching Chandler's vehicle as it pulled into the parking lot of a Lake City car stereo store, but the aerial crew had to leave their post due to strong wind and heavy rain from the thunderstorm. By the time ground units in unmarked cars could respond to the parking lot, Chandler's vehicle was gone.

Investigators feared they might have lost their only chance. They had no idea where Chandler was until a week later on September 24 when he called his Port Orange home from a payphone just off I-75 in Valdosta, Georgia, near the Florida state line. He had gone to Kentucky and Ohio to pawn stolen jewelry and was now driving back home.

After receiving word of the 2:30 p.m. call to Chandler's house, FBI and FDLE task force members scrambled to take him down. Shortly after 6:00 p.m., Chandler pulled his blue Corolla into at a gas station off I-95 in Port Orange. As Chandler filled his car's gas tank, FDLE Agent John Halliday crept up behind him with his gun drawn. When Halliday announced that he was under arrest for sexual battery in the Madeira Beach rape case, Chandler did not act surprised. It was as if he had been expecting it.

"Oba Chandler, you're under arrest," Halliday said.

"What for?" Chandler asked.

"Rape," Halliday replied.

"Ok," Chandler said as Halliday helped him into the backseat of a police car.

After so many months trying to solve the case and imagining what the mysterious killer would look like, Detective Cummings was disappointed. Dressed in a pullover shirt and jeans and visibly tired from the long drive, the 45-year-old, 6-

foot-tall, 190-pound Chandler looking nothing like the monster she imagined.

"He looked like just another dirtbag," she said.

Still going by the name James Wright, Chandler had been living with his wife and 3-year-old daughter in "The Woods," a middle-class neighborhood dotted with oak trees, well-maintained lawns, and Crime Watch stickers. Following the arrest, a resident of The Woods pointed out that it was a "very quiet neighborhood" and a "perfect place to hide out."

As news of the arrest circulated, Chandler's neighbors expressed surprise.

"They seemed like a nice American family," Chuck Copeland shared. "He was always smiling, always playing with his little girl."

Twin fifteen-year-old girls who lived in the neighborhood frequently babysat Chandler's young daughter, and Steve Jurkowski recalled how Chandler had come to his aid when Jurkowski's truck got stuck in mud. Using his own Jeep Cherokee, Chandler towed Jurkowski's truck from the muck.

"It was real neighborly of him," Jurkowski said of his "friendly and outgoing" neighbor. "He seemed like a normal guy. I always saw good things. It's hard to comprehend."

Another neighbor, Rita Mehegan, remembered how Chandler had invited her son to go fishing with him.

"He is just a nice, normal guy," she said.

Tim and Maria Pearson, Chandler's next-door neighbors, heard about the arrest on the 11 o'clock news and could not believe their ears. Chandler had been a model neighbor to them. He was someone they could always rely on to lend a helping hand, whether it be for replacing their front walk or repairing their pool pump.

"We would never have suspected someone like Oba – we called him Obie. Of all the neighbors in the area, he was the one we'd least suspect."

Port Orange Police Chief Bob Ford gave a similar report about the Chandler family.

"We heard nothing about them. No calls. No complaints. No barking dog. Nothing."

However, one resident insisted that he had always suspected something was not right about Chandler.

"The way the man carried himself in the neighborhood, he struck me as a con man," said Tom Mehegan. "Quite honestly, I didn't like him from the time I saw him."

Noting how close Chandler fit the psychological profile prepared by the FBI, Detective Moore confirmed that those who knew him provided consistent feedback about his pleasant personality and friendly demeanor.

"He's a very nice person, that's the indication we get from people who know him . . . He fits all the things we said he would be."

Longtime FBI agent John Douglas, used as a model for the character Jack Crawford in the film adaptation of *The Silence of the Lambs*, expressed satisfaction with the degree of accuracy that his unit's psychological profile had achieved with regard to Chandler.

"We're not the ones who are knocking down doors and making arrests," Douglas said, "but if we contribute in a small way to the identification and apprehension of a suspect, it's very rewarding. It keeps you going, particularly in cases like this." He called the Rogers investigation a "very unique case," and felt an ambivalent reaction to the arrest, finding it simultaneously "very sad, but very rewarding."

～

Shortly before midnight, an unmarked police car pulled up to the Pinellas County Jail in St. Petersburg. Two police officers led the stocky, well-groomed Chandler, clad in blue jeans and a paisley print shirt, past a crowd of 20 reporters gathered at the entrance before booking him into the jail, where he was held on a $1 million bail. For his protection, Chandler was assigned to the jail's B-Wing where he would be separated from the general inmate population and be monitored by jail officials around-the-clock.

Back in Ohio, Hal Rogers expressed guarded optimism about the arrest.

"I hope it is the guy," he said. "It's been so damn long and you go up and down so many times, you don't get excited about anything anymore. I guess you could say I have kind of a cavalier attitude about it – I have to."

～

The last week of September brought a flurry of activity in the case. On September 25, agents from the Florida Department of Law Enforcement, the FBI, and St. Petersburg Police Department searched Chandler's Port Orange home. They found two trunks full of $250,000 worth of jewelry along with jeweler tools, video tapes of sexual bondage, and a green mesh shirt like the one Jan Bradley had described her rapist as wearing.

The next day, Assistant Public Defender Ronald Eide called the $1-million bond set for Chandler "absurd." Although the large bond had clearly been imposed with the Rogers murders in mind, Eide planned to request a reduction since the amount "doesn't make any sense on a sexual battery charge" and even a $100,000 bond "would be unusual."

Eide also discounted the FDLE expert's opinion that the handwriting on the Clearwater Beach brochure was Chandler's.

"What does handwriting prove?" he asked, calling such analysis an "inexact science."

A reporter asked Detective Moore why police named Chandler as a suspect without formally charging him with the Rogers murders. The reporter brought up the 1990 investigation into the Gainesville Ripper murders in which Gainesville police had mistakenly named Edward Humphrey as a suspect.

"It's an easy question to answer," Moore replied. "You all would have gone ahead and said it, if we didn't. We're continuing to work on the case. Our main emphasis was to get him off the street."

Citing the belief that Chandler traveled extensively along the East Coast of the country, Moore released a nationwide police bulletin describing Chandler's arrest to see if he could be tied to any unsolved crimes in other jurisdictions. Since his arrest about 60 people had called the St. Petersburg Police Department about Chandler, including half a dozen female callers who claimed that he tried to get them alone on his boat.

To end out the week, Symphony Pictures, a Los Angeles production company, expressed interest in producing a movie about the Rogers case, which would focus on Pinellas County Commissioner Barbara Todd's role in finding the killer.

"We like to do stories where women are the heroes, and women help solve crimes," said producer Gary Caloroso. "We like to do stories that promote strength in females, and we have a hero here in Barbara."

Todd had come up with the idea of displaying the Clearwater Beach handwritten directions on billboards because she had been so troubled by the police's inability to catch the killer that she was having trouble sleeping at night.

"I thought if his handwriting is so unique, like they said it was, why not blow it up and let everyone look at it?" Todd explained. "This was such a strange idea," she admitted, "but I knew if I didn't do it, he wasn't going to get caught. I could not bear the thought that another woman would suffer at the hands of this monster."

Like Joan Rogers, Todd was a mother with daughters. That made the murders even more troubling.

"This particular thing has haunted me, because I have

young girls and it bothered me that somebody like this would be running around our community. Here they are guests in our community and they meet such a heinous fate. We wanted this killer caught."

PHOTOS

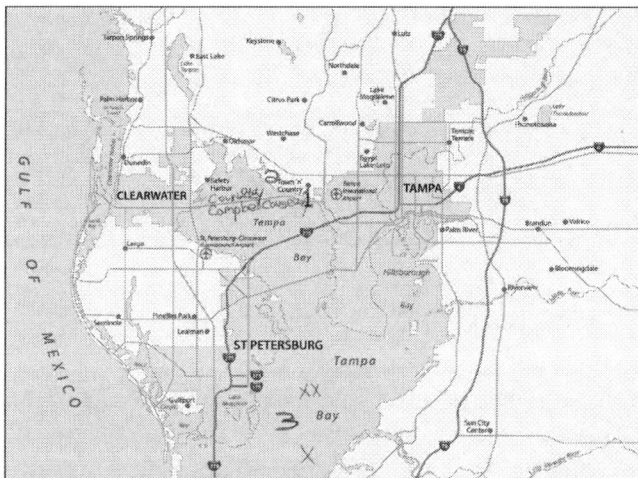

Map of the Tampa Bay Area

1. Boat ramp where Joan Rogers's car was found
2. Home owned by Oba Chandler in 1989 at time of Rogers murders
3. Area where Rogers' bodies were found (X = 1st body; XX = 2nd & 3rd)

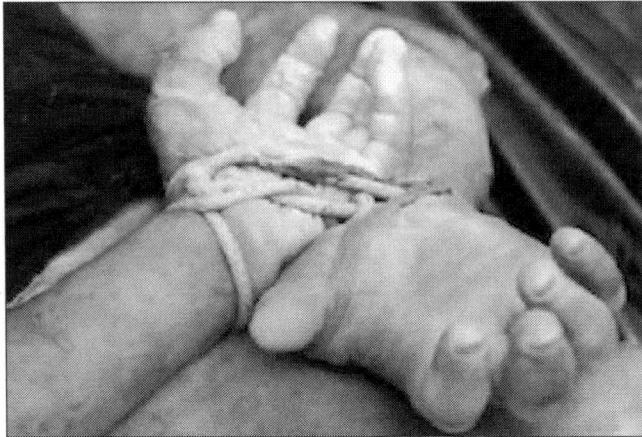
Bound hands of one of the bodies found in
Tampa Bay (SPPD)

Body bag containing one of the victims after
their transport to the Coast Guard station
(SPPD)

Christe Rogers (SPPD)

Michelle Rogers (SPPD)

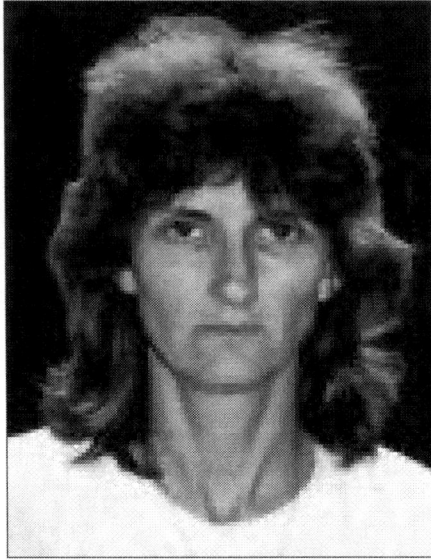

Joan Rogers (SPPD)

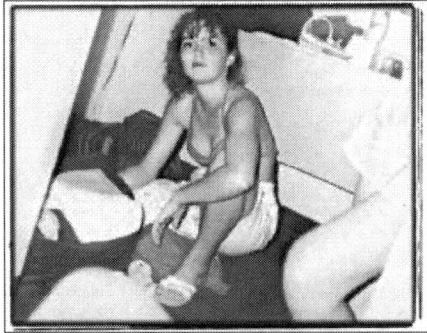

Michelle Rogers sitting in Room 251 of the Days Inn motel at Rocky Point only a few hours before the Rogers' disappearance (SPPD)

The last shot on a roll of camera film found in the Rogers' motel room. The photo shows the view from the balcony of their second-floor room (SPPD)

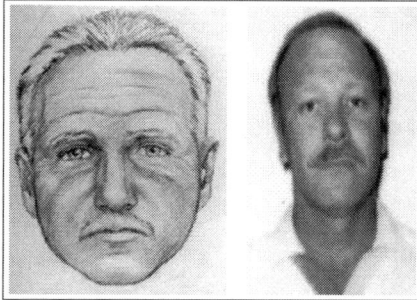

Composite sketch of the suspect in the Madeira Beach rape case next to a photograph of what Oba Chandler looked like at the time (SPPD)

WHO KILLED THE ROGERS FAMILY?
ON THURSDAY, JUNE 1, 1989

$25,000 REWARD FOR ARREST AND CONVICTION
ST PETERSBURG POLICE DEPT 893-7104

One of the billboards that police erected around the Tampa Bay area in an effort to generate new leads in the Rogers case (SPPD)

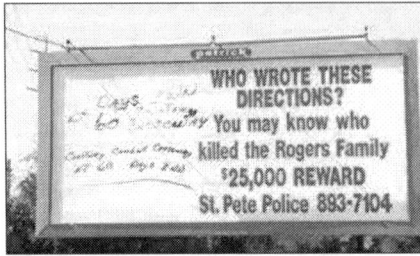

Billboard that police erected at the suggestion of Commissioner Barbara Todd with blow-up of the handwritten directions on the Clearwater Beach tourist brochure found in the Rogers' car (SPPD)

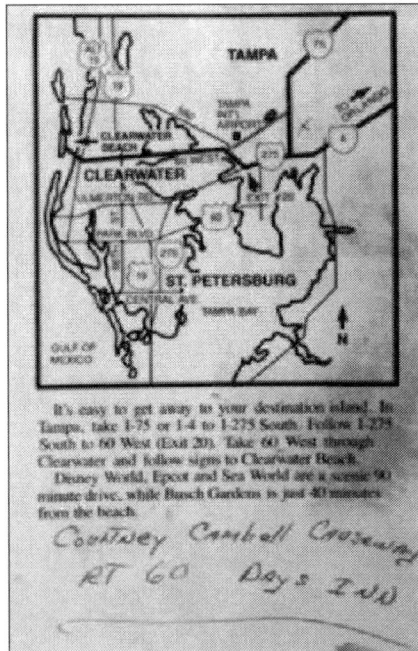

Part of the Clearwater Beach tourist brochure with a small map of the Tampa Bay area and handwritten directions below it (SPPD)

Oba Chandler during his criminal trial for the triple homicide of Joan, Michelle, and Christe Rogers

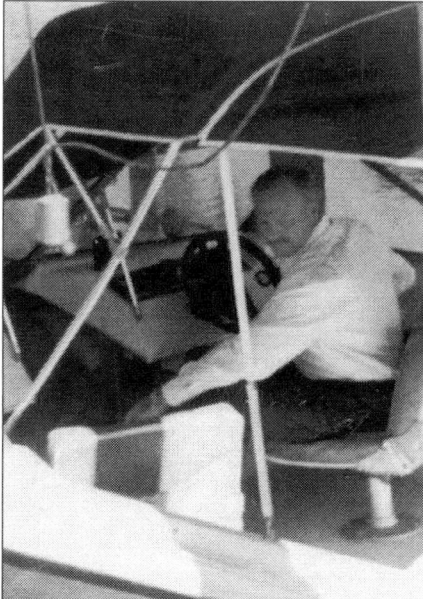

Oba Chandler on board his boat, *Gypsy I*, around the time of the Madeira Beach rape and Rogers' murders (SPPD)

Chandler's boat used in the Madeira Beach
rape and Rogers' murders (SPPD)

View at night from an area near where the
Rogers women were likely thrown overboard.
Lights of buildings on the distant shore show
how far the Rogers were from any potential
help (Pinellas County State Attorney Office
Investigator)

Oba Chandler
LAST STATEMENT

You are Killing a innocent man
Today

Nov. 15th 2011

Oba Chandler

Last statement of Oba Chandler that he
handwrote the day of his execution (FDOC)

Ivelisse Berrios Beguerisse (20) abducted and
murdered in Broward County, Florida on
November 27, 1990 (CSPD)

Beguerisse's car found in the Sawgrass Mills Mall parking lot with both passenger side tires deflated by knife puncture. Her nude body was found in a residential neighborhood in Coral Springs (CSPD)

SEVENTEEN

To ensure that Chandler remained behind bars while the Rogers triple homicide investigation continued, prosecutors charged him with robbery with a firearm in connection with the September 11 robbery of two jewelers in Pinellas Park. Following Chandler's arrest for the Madeira Beach rape, investigators had learned more details about the Pinellas Park robbery by interrogating his wife, Debra.

Debra explained that Oba had prepared for the crime by showing her a Days Inn where he would meet her after the robbery, then he had her drop him off at the Pinellas Park Residence Inn at 9:30 p.m. Debra followed his instructions to park their car at the back of the Residence Inn with the plan to follow him to the Days Inn whenever he drove past her. She had barely starting reading a story to their 3-year-old daughter,

Whitney, when Chandler pulled up driving the jewelers' stolen rental car.

"All I had time to do was park the car under the light, pick up the book and start reading her the story, and he came around the corner in a different car," Debra told detectives. "All I had time to do is throw the book down, start the car, and follow him," she said, describing what happened next. At the Days Inn, Chandler took three large brief cases out of the trunk of the stolen vehicle and put them in Debra's car. Then they drove back to their Port Orange home. Along with all of the jewelry, Chandler found a jeweler's blowtorch in one of the cases from the robbery.

"He melted down the gold and took that to some company in Orlando and gave me some, so, you know, that I would have some money," she told investigators.

About a week later, Chandler sold and traded the rest of the jewelry in Hazard, Kentucky during the town's annual Black Gold Festival.

He left for that trip, "and I never saw him again," Debra Chandler explained.

Debra had some extra incentive to work with detectives. In April 1990, while working for Alumco Industries of Clearwater, she had provided $7000 worth of aluminum to her husband and falsely marked the bills as paid. Due to those actions, she faced four counts of grand theft.

Debra also revealed that in early November 1989, Chandler left home without telling her where he was going. It was shortly after he had seen the composite sketch of the Madeira Beach rapist on the news, and he fled Florida for the familiar safety of his home-state of Ohio.

~

On October 8, Oba Chandler's sister, Lula Harris, told prosecutors that Debra confided in her that she suspected him of having some involvement with the Rogers murders.

"She was scared because she was afraid he did do it," Harris said. "She was frightened because he was saving the [newspaper] clippings."

Harris had also seen the clippings herself on one occasion on a counter in Chandler's house.

~

During a tape-recorded telephone conversation from jail with his daughter, Kristal Mays, Chandler denied killing the Rogers women:

> I know I've had a lot of problems in my life, you know. I know I've done things that I shouldn't have done, but I have never physically hurt no human being in my life. Never. Everything I've always done has just been con games and things like that, you know what I mean.

He also denied ever telling anyone that he had killed the

three Rogers women, asking Mays if she would admit that to anyone.

"If I killed three people, would I tell somebody?" Mays asked in reply.

"Yeah, would you tell somebody," Chandler replied. "No. Nobody would."

~

On November 10, after three hours of deliberation, a Pinellas grand jury indicted Chandler on three charges of first-degree murder in the Rogers case.

Members of his family reacted to the grand jury's decision with mixed emotions ranging from reluctant acceptance to outright disbelief.

"I was hoping it wasn't true," said his sister Lula Harris. "No matter what he does, I'll still love him with all my heart. Even though I know he's done these things, I don't hate him. He's my brother, and he's part of me."

Chandler's mother reacted with denial.

"He didn't do that murder," she insisted. "He didn't do it, I know he didn't. I never knowed him to hurt a hair on anyone's head."

His sister, Alma, shared their mother's sentiment.

"If I thought he was guilty I would be the first one to say so,"Alma said. "In my heart and soul, I know he is not capable of that kind of violence."

Detective Moore believed differently.

"This guy traveled. He was on the prowl all the time," Moore asserted. "He is just like any of these other types of killers. Ted Bundy or anyone else. They go out on the prowl to find their victim."

One such prowling may have happened in Daytona Beach in 1991 when a 15-year-old girl was approached by a man driving a van. The girl thought that the man wanted directions, but when she came closer to his vehicle he jumped out, grabbed her arm, and dragged her into the van. After getting her inside his van, the man bound the girl's wrists and ankles with duct tape as she screamed and struggled. When she would not heed his warnings to stop making noise, he pressed his hand over her mouth and choked her, then taped her mouth shut. Having subdued her, the man fondled her breasts before driving away with her bound and gagged in the back. As the man drove her toward an unknown destination, the girl struggled against her restraints and eventually freed herself. Before her abductor realized what was happening, she jumped from the van's window. Although she broke her foot while jumping from the moving vehicle, she was able to flee and find help.

~

As the case continued toward trial, JJ Geoghegan marveled at everything that had happened in order for Chandler to be caught.

"It was very frustrating. Everyone was a potential suspect," Geoghegan said, thinking back to the beginning of the investigation. "It could have been a doctor, a lawyer, a judge or a street person. Nobody was above suspicion."

It did not help that many of the leads that had been phoned in came from ulterior motives, causing investigators to spend countless hours spinning their wheels.

"There were people who used police to cause problems for other people. We'd get what we thought was a good suspect until we'd learn it couldn't be him. We wasted a lot of time on those people."

Over 20,000 hours of investigative time had been spent by the end of the second year of the investigation.

"It was all-consuming," Geoghegan acknowledged.

Despite the wild goose chase prompted by tipsters with their own agendas, Geoghegan remained thankful for the public's participation in the lengthy investigatory process. The fact that all those thousands of hours of investigation very likely would have been for naught, but for a few members of the public, was not lost on him.

"This case shows that a persistent, suspicious neighbor solved a triple murder by getting involved. Police can't always do it alone. If more people got involved, we'd solve more cases."

And he singled out one member of the public in particular as instrumental in identifying the Rogers' likely killer.

"Ms. Steffey was key to solving this case," he asserted. "That woman did fantastic police work before she ever called us. She was suspicious, but cautious . . . I told her, 'I'd take you as a partner in a heartbeat,'" he said with a smile.

As investigators gathered more information about

Chandler and his whereabouts over the years, they became convinced that he was a serial rapist and killer, and it solidified Geoghegan's belief that they were dealing with a seasoned killer.

"We always thought that this man's a serial killer. You don't start off killing three people. You work up to that."

Among other rapes detectives now suspected Chandler of committing were an unreported rape in Pinellas Park in 1963, sex with an underage girl in Cincinnati in 1964, an attempted rape in Cincinnati in 1965, an unreported rape in Daytona Beach in 1973, and unreported rape in Pasco County in 1990.

"We have several rape cases confirmed and we feel confident that we're going to have some other homicides," Moore said. "We don't yet know the full extent of his other activities just like with Ted Bundy – they knew only about a few things until before he was executed."

That Chandler's former wives had told investigators that he would suddenly disappear at times – sometimes for more than a month – seemed to support Moore's belief in the extent of Chandler's proclivity for crime.

"We won't know the final chapters on him for a while," Moore predicted.

EIGHTEEN

While Detective Moore's assertion concerning the final chapters about Oba Chandler foreshadowed the future, investigators now knew much more about his past.

～

Oba Chandler was born on October 11, 1946, in Cincinnati General Hospital in Cincinnati, Ohio. His father, Oba William Chandler, claimed to be a full-blooded Indian of Cherokee and Lakota descent. Chandler Sr. grew up in a poor coal-mining family in Breathitt County in eastern Kentucky. He moved to Cincinnati with his second wife, Margaret Johnson, when Oba was a boy. Oba Sr. took a job as a laborer for National Distillers and Chemical Co. and the family rented a small house in Cincinnati on Clay Street in a blue-collar neighborhood near downtown. Oba Sr. set strict rules for Oba and his four sisters. "You don't lie, you don't steal, you don't cheat," was the motto he drilled into them repeatedly. He was quick to punish when they disobeyed him, usually by whipping them with his leather razor strop.

On May 31, 1957, Oba Sr. hung himself in the basement of his Cincinnati home with a half-inch thick rope. He had been depressed over the death of one of his sons in a power line accident, and the family had a history of suicide. Oba Sr.'s brother and sister had both killed themselves well before he took his own life.

The next day, 10-year-old Oba Jr. walked up a steep hillside to the cemetery for his father's burial. Oba Sr.'s death hit him hard. His cousin, Elizabeth Noble, later recalled how when the gravediggers began shoveling dirt into his father's grave, Oba Jr. jumped in, stood on top of the coffin, and stomped the dirt down while muttering "He didn't have to do that."

~

Whether Noble's recollection is accurate or not, the impact of Oba Sr.'s suicide on his 10-year-old son should not be underestimated. In 2021, Amy Renee, a poster who learned about the suicide on a true crime website, wrote about a very similar reaction she had when *her* father killed himself:

> *When Oba's father hung himself and he then jumped onto the casket, I could totally relate to that. My dad shot himself in the*

head one month after I turned 18, and we had a private family viewing, during that viewing I apparently started to scream and flip out while crying and I started to climb into the casket with my dad. It took three grown men to pull me out. I lost it. Before he killed himself, I had a life plan, I had a bright future . . . But I completely went off track. I didn't start committing major crimes, but I started taking prescription meds incorrectly and drinking, and making poor choices. Having that type of trauma as a child, can absolutely damage you. I am now 37, and I am doing significantly better, but it took me nearly 15 years to get myself on the right track. I feel for anyone that goes through that. Granted, we are still responsible for our own decisions, but it changes you.

~

After his father's death, Oba began hanging around a group of delinquent boys, stole a neighbor's bike, and used his BB gun to shoot at cars. When he was 14, he stole a car to go joyriding, the start of a series of poor choices that led him to appear in juvenile court nearly twenty times before he turned 18.

In 1960, Chandler moved out of his parents' home and moved in with his sister Helen in Tampa, who then shuffled him off to his sister Alma in Pinellas Park. He enrolled in Pinellas Park Middle School for 9th grade in October, but then withdrew for below average grades and returned to Cincinnati. He came back to Pinellas County in 1963, this time with his mother and step-father. Over the next two years, he fathered three children – Kristal, Valerie, and Jeffrey – with two different women.

In December 1965, Chandler enlisted in the United States Marine Corps. During boot camp at Camp Lejeune, North Carolina, he received training in antitank assault and sharpshooting. He served at Paris Island, South Carolina, but a month after joining, he received a court-marshal for disobeying the commands of a Lieutenant and Sergeant. After being found guilty and sentenced to 30 days of hard labor, he was honorably discharged in January 1967.

In February 1969, police found 21 women's wigs worth $1,300 in Chandler's possession. The wigs had been stolen from Rita's Beauty Room the month before. The following year in Bond Hill, Ohio, he abandoned his wife and two daughters, including 7-year-old Kristal Mays, and he moved to St. Paul, Minnesota, where he fathered another son, Skipper.

On March 1, 1971, Chandler was arrested for exposing himself and masturbating in front of an apartment building in Cincinnati. His Probation & Parole evaluator recorded that Chandler's attitude "continues to be one of manipulation. He attempts to get by with all he can."

In 1976, Chandler broke into a home in Holly Hill, Florida near Daytona Beach in Volusia County, and tied up Robert Plemmons and his girlfriend with speaker wire and telephone cords. Chandler had targeted them when the saw Plemmons take a large amount of money out of his pocket while negotiating the price of a boat at a boat show. Driving a black van with a mural on the side depicting a motorcyclist in a graveyard, Chandler followed Plemmons from the boat show to his house.

The next night, Chandler and an accomplice returned to the house and knocked on the front door, pretending to be out of gas. As Plemmons started to unlatch the door, Chandler kicked it in, brandished a gun, and ordered Clemmons to lay on the ground while his accomplice tied him up. Once Plemmons was immobilized, Chandler dragged his girlfriend into the bedroom, ordered her to strip to her underwear, and tied her up with telephone cords. After forcing her to lay on the bed, he rubbed the barrel of his revolver across her stomach. Chandler and his accomplice eventually fled, taking the couple's Doberman pinscher, a rifle, and a handgun along with some cash.

Captured and charged with kidnapping, armed robbery, and burglary, Chandler pled guilty to a single count of robbery on January 12, 1977, and received a sentence of 10 years imprisonment. Prison officials evaluating Chandler concluded that he "appears to have superior learning aptitude with higher than average educational achievement" and noted he had an above average IQ of 120.

Chandler's prison stay did not last long. On May 10, 1977, he escaped from Doctors Inlet Road Prison, a state prison camp near Jacksonville, FL, by walking away from a medium-security prison crew doing road work along I-95.

Chandler obtained a Florida driver's license with the name James Wright and the following year "James Wright" was arrested in Altamonte Springs for loitering and prowling. A startled woman discovered him staring at her when she looked out the bedroom window of her apartment at 2:30 a.m.

In 1979, Chandler (Wright) was arrested for prowling near an apartment complex in Orange County that had been hit with a series of burglaries. Another arrest came in July 1981 for tampering with a coin machine by using a coat hanger to break into the coin box of a soda dispenser. Chandler subsequently became a confidential informant for the Orlando Metropolitan Bureau of Investigations using his alias of James Wright, an ironic deceit he clearly relished since he would undertake a similar ruse in the future.

On June 15, 1982, Randal Murphy and Diane Hickey were arrested for passing counterfeit $20 bills at the World's Fair in Knoxville, Tennessee. They informed the arresting agents that they had been picked up by a man named "Jim" outside Ocala, Florida, and he ended up giving them $200 in the counterfeit bills. They claimed that Jim had approximately $7,500 of the bills in his car, a brown Toyota hatchback.

The evening of September 27, U.S. Secret Service agents arrested 35-year-old "James Wright" as he was driving through an intersection on Maitland Boulevard in Maitland, Florida. They staked out his house, then followed him as he drove off. At an intersection they blocked in his car with their vehicles and arrested him at gun point. During the arrest, Agent Robert Connelly noticed that Chandler seemed "very nervous and very scared."

Agents found $8,430 in counterfeit $20 bills in his car. Chandler told them that he had obtained the bills from his uncle, Ralph Johnson, in Holly Hill, Florida, who gave him approximately $50,000 of them.

At time of his arrest, Chandler "lived two lives," one as a wanted man at large for more than five years, and another as an aluminum siding contractor. He lived in a two-story home with his girlfriend and two large Dobermans, named "Adam" and "Eve," in a quiet neighborhood lined with brick streets near downtown Orlando.

Neighbors were shocked to learn of "James Wright's" arrest. "You never think anybody next door would be that way," neighbor Doug Jones said. "He seemed like a nice guy. Now I understand why he had two Dobermans."

In October, still using his alias James Wright, Chandler entered a plea agreement in federal court on counterfeiting charges. On November 29, 1982, he was sentenced to seven years in federal prison and subsequently served his time in Texas and Florida.

While incarcerated for counterfeiting, Chandler wrote a letter to federal judge John A. Reed, asking for a reduced sentence. He told the judge how he had worked for adult book stores while a fugitive and that "due to my help" authorities shut down some of the stores. He also highlighted his education while in prison – having earned his GED and 33 credits towards an associate's degree – and mentioned his recent reunion with his two daughters and desire to spend time with his seven grandchildren.

*Sir, during the time that I was an escapee from the Florida penal
system, I lived a quiet life . . . I was going to turn myself in as
soon as my Girlfriend completed school to finish my time in Fla. I
never had a moment's peace of mind since I exscaped (sic) from a
road Gang in Jacksonville. Judge Reed, I need this chance in my
life to keep the things I've worked for these last five years . . . I am
now 40 years old and a very changed person from who I was 10
years ago. I know I will have no type of trouble upon my release. .
.I will never get in trouble again.*

Chandler's assurance that he would stay out of trouble did
not sway Judge Reed, who denied his request for a reduced
sentence. Moreover, in 1984 a Jacksonville circuit court judge
sentenced Chandler to an additional six months imprisonment
in the Duval County Jail as punishment for his 1977 prison
work crew escape.

Chandler was released from prison on December 12, 1986,
and on May 14, 1988, he married Debra Whiteman of Tarpon
Springs, who had divorced her previous husband just ten days
earlier. Chandler cut ties of his own to go forward with the
marriage. While dating Debra, he had been living with and
engaged to another woman, Barbara Leiby.

In November 1988, Chandler and his latest wife purchased
a single-story, tan-colored, three-bedroom, stucco house in the
Tampa Shores subdivision, near the top of Old Tampa Bay.
They moved into the house at 10709 Dalton Avenue in
December. The house had a pool in the backyard, backed onto
a canal leading to Tampa Bay, and had two davits for lowering

and raising boats. They used $10,000 of Debra's $40,000 divorce settlement from her first husband as the down payment. As part of the deal, they bought the owner's powerboat, a 21-foot Bayliner, for a hundred dollars. The German man who sold them the house and boat had named the boat "Zigeuner," German for "Gypsy".

Oba and Debra's daughter, Whitney, was born on February 6, 1989.

In July 1990, Oba and Debra Chandler told neighbors they were moving to California, but in September, they leased an apartment at 11600 NW 33rd Street in Sunrise, a city in the southeastern part of the state. They lived in Sunrise for only a short time before relocating to Port Orange, Oba's final residence before being taken into custody.

NINETEEN

On July 29, 1993, in response to Oba Chandler's request that his triple-murder trial be moved from Pinellas County to Hillsborough County, the Florida Supreme Court appointed Pinellas-Pasco Circuit Judge Susan Schaeffer to serve as judge in the proceedings. A lawyer since graduating from Stetson University in 1971, Schaeffer had been a judge since 1984, and she had a reputation as a no-nonsense jurist with a sharp legal mind.

In October, the court appointed Fred Zinober, a commercial litigation attorney and former assistant state attorney, to be lead defense counsel for Chandler. A true crime afficionado, Zinober did not want to pass up "one of those cases that may come along once in your life." He agreed to take the case for a flat fee much less than what his normal hourly rate would command. Known for immersing himself in the cases he litigated, Zinober booked a room at the Gateway Inn – the same hotel that the Rogers family had stayed in – when depositions were taken in Orlando.

"I got a sense of, this was the last place they had been before they came to Tampa and were killed. What is it that they saw? It's kind of like you're living a true crime novel," he noted.

After reviewing the police files for the Rogers case, Zinober became convinced that he could successfully defend Chandler against the three murder charges despite the vast resources of the State Attorney's Office being deployed to prosecute the case. He not-so-secretly relished the role of underdog in the David versus Goliath contest.

"It's not an easy case," he conceded. "Sometimes I feel like I'm fighting the Russian army with a water gun. But I'm not afraid of that."

On November 10, with his trial for the Rogers murders still pending, Chandler was transported from the Hillsborough County Jail to Daytona Beach to face more robbery charges, these stemming from a 1991 robbery. With his ankles and hands in chains, Chandler pleaded not guilty to charges that he robbed Sally Wurmnest of $150,000 in jewelry, $16,000 in cash, a .38-caliber Smith & Wesson handgun, and her 1985 Dodge van.

About six months after Fred Zinober's appointment as lead defense counsel, the State Attorney's Office tapped Executive Assistant State Attorney Doug Crow, a lawyer with over 20 years of experience and a reputation for bulldog tenacity, to lead the prosecution team for trial. Crow had been the prosecutor on duty back in June 1989 when Joan, Michelle, and Christe's bodies were fished out of the bay. He remembered the day vividly and he wanted to be the one who helped put Oba Chandler away. The importance of the Rogers case to the State Attorney's Office became clear from the very beginning. Instead of the usual two attorneys for a murder trial, Chandler's trial would have four prosecutors with Crow being in charge.

During pretrial depositions Crow questioned Debra Chandler about her husband's activities and whereabouts on the night of the Rogers murders, as well as the night of the Madeira Beach rape.

"Can you provide an alibi of any sort as to where he was?" Crow asked.

"I do not recall where he was on that date," she replied despite knowing that the information requested would be extremely important if she hoped to bolster her husband's defense against the three murder charges. Crow pressed her on the issue.

"Can you give me any information, whether it would incriminate your husband or exculpate him, as to his whereabouts on the day of the rape and the days surrounding the murder?" Crow inquired.

"No, I can't," she insisted.

Crow asked her if she had attempted to remember *anything* about the days surrounding the rape and the three murders.

"No, I have not," she said gruffly, "I'm trying to block that out."

~

In June 1994, the State Attorney's Office released phone records it had subpoenaed from GTE that placed Chandler on his boat in Tampa Bay the night of the Rogers killings. The records revealed that five calls were made from the VHF radio on Chandler's boat, *Gypsy I*, to his home on Dalton Avenue. The first call, which lasted for about five minutes, was placed at 1:12 a.m. on June 2 and the last one was at 9:52 a.m. For the final call, the marine operator noted that the caller identified himself as "Oba". The records also showed that a call had been placed from Chandler's boat at 5:49 p.m. on the night of the Madeira Beach rape.

The next month prosecutors filed pretrial documents that included statements by inmate Dennis Rowe, who had been arrested for robbery in September 1992, and spent over a week in the same cell as Chandler. Rowe claimed that Chandler told him he had a "buddy" hiding on board his boat when he picked up Joan, Michelle, and Christe Rogers. When the friend revealed himself after they were out in the bay, Joan became upset.

Chandler threatened to throw the three women into the bay and when Joan responded, "Well, I think you're too much of a gentleman for that," Chandler replied by laughing. Then he struck Joan in the head and knocked her out. His buddy grabbed Michelle and said, "This one is mine," while Chandler, brandishing a fillet knife, raped Christe at knifepoint.

After the rapes were over, Chandler tied concrete blocks to

all three women and threw them overboard, mockingly telling them to "swim for it." According to Rowe, Chandler had to replace the carpeting in his boat afterward because Michelle threw up on it. Rowe also claimed that while in jail he overheard Chandler tell his "buddy" to dispose of evidence that would connect him to the crimes.

Rowe said Chandler met the three Rogers women at a gas station.

"They was looking for the mall," Rowe stated. "The younger girl had a camera and was having trouble getting the film in. He helped her with it. The mother walked up and they started talking."

Chandler hit it off with Joan when she learned they were both from Ohio.

"They told him they planned on going to the beach to get photos of the sunset for their dad. That's when he told them he had a boat, and invited them for a cruise."

When they showed up at the boat ramp at 5:00 p.m., Chandler helped them carry a cooler and two bags aboard.

Although Dennis Rowe's statements seemed to bolster the prosecution's case against Chandler, a decision by Judge Schaeffer ensured prosecutors would not be in an exuberant mood. In a mixed-bag ruling, the judge determined that prosecutors could use evidence from the Madeira Beach rape case in Chandler's triple-murder trial. However, if they chose to do so then they could not have Rowe testify about Chandler's alleged confession because Rowe's account of the killings differed too much from what Jan Bradley had described in the Madeira Beach case.

On August 11, in one of the last pretrial depositions taken by prosecutors, Rick Mays, Chandler's son-in-law, testified that Chandler drove him around the Tampa Bay area when he visited Chandler in the summer of 1989. According to Mays, as Chandler drove over the bridge at John's Pass, he pointed out the dock as a place where he picked up a woman he raped, and also boasted to him that "I picked up a couple of women" somewhere else and raped them.

"He said sex was any place you wanted it," Mays testified. "Everywhere he went, sex was there . . . Sex was all over Florida, all you had to do was stick out your hand and point your finger and come on and you had it."

Mays's testimony about Chandler's words painted the picture of a man with a narcissistic personality and suggested that even darker psychological disorders lurked underneath.

PART III

"The truth is criminals sometimes make mistakes, or we would never catch them. They don't commit perfect crimes."

– Executive Assistant State Attorney Doug Crow

TWENTY

More than five years after the murders of Joan, Michelle, and Christe Rogers, their triple homicide case came to be heard in court. Oba Chandler's trial on three counts of first-degree murder began at 8:30 a.m. on Monday morning, September 19, 1994, in Courtroom M, the largest courtroom of the Criminal Courts Complex in Clearwater. It was not Judge Susan Schaeffer's normal courtroom, but the widespread publicity of the case required her to borrow the larger space to accommodate all of the media and members of the public who wanted to watch.

To lessen the chance of undue influence from pretrial media coverage of the case, the 12 jurors and two alternates had been chosen from a 350-person jury pool in Orlando and then brought to Pinellas County for the trial pursuant to a newly enacted state law. Chandler's trial was the first time a court put the new law to use. During the remarkably fast two-day jury selection, defense attorney Fred Zinober had warned prospective jurors that it would be "an emotional case" and they would likely be shown disturbing photographs of Joan, Michelle, and Christe Rogers' bodies. The nine female and five male jurors ultimately chosen to decide the question of Chandler's guilt included a minister's wife, a missile mechanic, two school bus drivers, three housewives, a hotel manager, UPS and USPS employees, and an apartment maintenance man.

Dressed in a button-down white shirt with red stripes and khakis, Chandler listened to the prosecution and defense attorneys' opening statements, at times jotting down notes on a legal pad, while other times holding his glasses in his hand and simply listening. Marking the beginning of what one reporter referred to as a case having "all the elements that make for a sensational trial: horrible murders, sex, and conspiracy theories," lead prosecutor Doug Crow told the jury members in his opening statement what proof to expect in a case that would necessarily rely on a web of circumstantial evidence. Since no direct evidence such as eyewitness testimony, DNA evidence, or another form of a smoking gun tied Chandler to the three homicides, the state would be relying on indirect evidence such as Chandler's handwriting on the Clearwater Beach travel brochure found in Joan Rogers's car, incriminating statements Chandler made to family members and fellow inmates, and records of maritime phone calls he made to his wife from onboard the *Gypsy I* in the predawn darkness of Tampa Bay.

As framed by Crow's account of the pertinent events,

Chandler's charisma and charm had overcome any reluctance or reservations Joan Rogers might have had about going out on a stranger's boat with her two daughters. Crow pointed to the boat as the key to the crime.

> Using a boat, under apparent cover of darkness, the killer committed a crime, miles out in the open water where there were no witnesses, save the dead victims, to see or hear or remember what happened.

And by using the boat, which then killer then removed and obviously cleaned up, he left no scene for the police to investigate.

During the defense's opening statement, Fred Zinober rejected the notion that Chandler – one man – could have killed three women on a 21-foot boat as alleged.

> You are going to ask: How can a man rape three women and throw them into the water from a boat this size?

. . . . .

> When the evidence is in on this case, you are going to reach the conclusion that this case is still an unsolved mystery.

After fighting during pretrial proceedings to keep any evidence of the Madeira Beach rape out of the triple-murder trial, Zinober surprised everyone by suddenly reversing his strategy:

> I'll tell you right now, ladies and gentlemen, that we are not here, and we are not going to defend the Madeira Beach rape case. That is a separate case.
>
> It is a totally different situation from our situation here. And although the facts are going to be presented by the State, I'm going to tell you right now that we are not defending the Madeira Beach rape case.
>
> You are going to find that the State is going to be able to prove beyond a reasonable doubt that person was Oba Chandler and that it was Oba Chandler that took Jan Matthews out in the boat. But the issues, I suggest, are going to be entirely different.
>
> . . . . .
>
> The defense in this case is very straight forward, very simple. It is simply that they have the wrong man.

Zinober promised the jury that Chandler himself would take the stand and testify about his innocence of any involvement in the Rogers murders.

"He's going to tell you from that witness stand, 'It's not me. They were not on my boat.'"

One of the first witnesses called in the trial, Edward

Corcoran, Associate Medical Examiner for Pinellas County and Pasco County, testified that he conducted autopsies of Joan, Michelle, and Christe Rogers on the same day that their bodies were found. Due to the decomposed condition of the bodies, Dr. Corcoran could not determine the specific cause of death of the three women, but he found evidence of both ligature strangulation and drowning. The bodies' state of decomposition also prevented him from determining whether they had been sexually assaulted since any semen would have quickly decomposed and been washed away by the action of the water. He estimated that they had been floating in the bay for two to three days before being discovered. The fact that there were no fractures of the hyoid bones indicated that the women had not been manually strangled to death.

Before the prosecution could call Hal Rogers to the witness stand, Zinober objected that allowing him to testify and then remain in the courtroom gallery to observe the rest of the trial would be unduly prejudicial:

> It's our position very vehemently that his presence in the courtroom after he testifies and now the jury knows who he is – and let's face it, this is a very disgusting homicide. This is the most emotional homicide I think any of us have ever been involved in. And to have him get on the stand and say who he is and sit there is just going to be overwhelmingly prejudicial to my client.

In response, Crow countered with the frank assessment that

"whether Mr. Rogers is sitting in the back of the courtroom or sitting outside the courtroom, the jury is certainly aware that his life has been devastated by total annihilation of his family."

After considering the two sides' positions, Judge Schaeffer overruled the defense objection, declaring that Hal Rogers "has a right to see what is going on in this case, to feel that whatever the verdict is, that the State Attorney has done their job, you have done your job, and that justice has been served, whatever that may be."

Clad in cowboy boots and a Western-cut suit, Hal Rogers described how the entire family helped work the dairy farm, with Joan and the two girls helping milk the farm's 75 Holstein dairy cows after they got home from work and school. He testified on direct examination that he had expected his wife and daughters to return home about a week after they left for their Florida vacation. The last time he heard from them had been the evening of Memorial Day when Joan called to let him know they were planning on going to Epcot Center and either MGM or Magic Kingdom.

When Crow asked Hal Rogers about a picture of Michelle in her prom dress, Zinober objected on relevance grounds, but the judge overruled his objection: "It's the State's position that this crime was sexually motivated, and the pictures they have introduced into evidence show me some ladies that would be quite attractive, perhaps sexually attractive, as opposed to some farm hands that may otherwise be depicted in pictures." Interestingly, Judge Schaeffer's comments seemed to run contrary to the generally recognized notion that power and control typically motivate rapists, rather than the sexual component of the rape.

~

On the second day of trial, Theresa Stubbs from the FDLE's Tampa Regional Crime Laboratory testified about her comparison of Chandler's handwriting from known samples to the words "Days Inn, Route 60, Courtney Causeway" written in pencil on the Clearwater Beach brochure. Stubbs opined that the handwriting matched, positively identifying Chandler as the person who wrote directions on the brochure. Although "no person writes precisely the same way twice," Stubbs found a consistent variation of the letters "C," "A", "R," and "Y," as well as a "consistent slant to the right" in the compared writings. Additionally, every time the letter "N" or "M" appeared in the writings it was capitalized, regardless of whether it was the first letter of the first word of a sentence.

Similarly, the distinctive capitalized "T" used in the brochure directions was used the same way in the middle of four words in a $2,776 work estimate written by Oba Chandler on June 5, 1990 for building a screen room in Tampa. The work estimate handwriting also contained several of the same "y" variations present in the brochure directions. Using the same technique of comparison to known handwriting samples, Stubbs also determined that the words "Boy Scout" and "Columbus" written in pen on a different part of the brochure were written by Joan Rogers.

Samuel McMullin, a latent-fingerprint examiner for the Hillsborough County Sheriff's Department, testified about his efforts in obtaining one latent palm print from the Clearwater Beach brochure. McMullin identified it as Oba Chandler's upon comparing it to prints he took from Chandler after his arrest.

The next day, Oba Chandler's 31-year-old daughter, Kristal Mays, testified that she first met her father in 1986 and saw him a few times over the next few years, including while staying at his house in Tampa during the last week of July 1989, only a month after the Rogers murders. Mays noticed rectangular-shaped concrete blocks laying on the ground along the side of the fence during that visit. She also told the jury about an unexpected visit that Chandler made to Cincinnati in November 1989.

That November 7 he had called her from an Econo Lodge motel in Cincinnati and asked her and her husband to come by. When they arrived at the motel, Chandler was "standing outside, waiting for us, and he was looking around." He seemed "anxious" and "appeared to be very nervous." She noticed that his Jeep, a dark navy blue 1985 Cherokee, was backed-in at a parking spot so that the license plate was nearly up against the building.

When Mays followed him into his room, she saw ashtrays all over the place that were "overflowing with cigarette butts." Throughout the visit, Chandler chain-smoked "cigarette after cigarette" and continued to act "very anxious and nervous." He told May that "he couldn't go back to Florida because they were looking for him for a rape of a woman." The next day, when Chandler came to her house, she overhead him tell her husband that he could not return to Florida because "the police were looking for him because he killed some women."

Kristal Mays's husband, James, followed her on the witness stand. He testified about Chandler's unexpected visit to Cincinnati again in 1990:

> He showed up at the door and said he ripped off the Coast Guard for some marijuana . . . and he wanted to know if I knew anybody that he could sell it to . . . he said he'd pay six thousand dollars to help him.

But after James set up the deal, Chandler robbed the buyers of $29,000 at gunpoint. When James tried to stop him, Chandler pointed the gun at him, gave him a "real cold look," and said, "Family don't mean shit to me."

After Kristal and James May's testimony, the state called Arthur Stephenson, an inmate in the Florida State Prison system with ten felony convictions. Stephenson testified that in late October and early November 1992, he served time in the same cell pod as Chandler. Stephenson and Chandler were the only occupants of the pod for three or four days, and during that time period the pod's TV showed news coverage of the Rogers case. While watching the coverage, Chandler told Stephenson that "he had met these women somewhere in the area of the stadium on Dale Mabry" and that he had given them directions to a boat ramp on the Courtney Campbell

Causeway. On a different occasion, when news coverage showed how the Rogers' bodies had been recovered from Tampa Bay, Chandler coyly remarked, "Well, that is something that they can't get me for. Dead people can't talk."

According to Stephenson, when Chandler met the Rogers, he quickly gained their trust after he learned that they were from Ohio. "Once something was said about them being from the same state, he seemed to take control of the situation and pretty much had them from that point." Chandler found Michelle Rogers very attractive from the moment he first saw her and he told Stephenson that she "turned him on."

Another inmate, William Katzer, testified that he shared a cell pod with Chandler in late January and early February 1993. One evening they saw coverage of the Rogers homicides on the television show, *A Current Affair*. According to Katzer, after the show ended, Chandler growled that "if the bitch didn't resist, I wouldn't be here."

A third inmate, Blake Leslie, testified that in the fall of 1992, he shared a cell in the Pinellas County Jail with Chandler. Leslie recalled a conversation with Chandler about the Madeira Beach rape in which Chandler said that he "took this young lady from another country for a ride in his boat" and "once he got out about twenty miles, thirty miles, he told her to 'fuck or swim.'" He also told Leslie that the "only reason the lady is still around is because somebody was waiting at the boat dock for her – one of her friends."

After the inmates testified, Robert Carlton recounted how he purchased Chandler's "spotless" boat for $5,000 in early

August 1989. Chandler took him out in the bay in it for a test drive and told him "how good the boat handled in rough water" and that he had "been out in the gulf with it, and it handled the rough water real good." He also mentioned that he frequently went night fishing and "knew how to navigate at night with his compass." When Carlton went to pick up the boat trailer from Chandler's yard, he noticed concrete blocks laying on it, "regular building blocks . . . like you build a house with."

～

The next day of trial, Rollins Cooper, a limited contractor who worked some jobs for Oba Chandler in the spring and summer of 1989, testified that he started one screen job for Chandler on May 31, but could not complete the job that day because Chandler had not delivered the materials needed to finish it. When Cooper returned to the job site on June 1, Chandler brought the material to the site between 11:00 a.m. and Noon.

Cooper noticed that Chandler seemed to be "in a hurry." When Cooper asked him why, Chandler told him that he "had a date with three women." The next morning, Cooper noticed that Chandler was "kind of grubby" and Chandler said that he had "been out on the boat all night."

On cross-examination, Zinober cited Cooper's deposition testimony from June 1993 to show that he had never before mentioned anything about Chandler's alleged statement of "having a date with three women." In response, Cooper asserted that he did not remember the statement until April

1994 when he woke up in the middle of the night. Zinober hoped the jury would be skeptical about Cooper's sudden recollection, and questioned him to call attention to the doubtful timing of it.

> **Zinober**: Okay. This is after you talked to law enforcement in person at least eight times?
>
> **Cooper**: Yes.
>
> **Zinober**: This is after you talked on the telephone with the State Attorney's Office at least five to fifteen times, right?
>
> **Cooper**: Yes.

~

The victim in the Madeira Beach rape case took the stand to finish the first week of trial. On Friday, September 23, Jan Bradley recounted how the man who introduced himself as Dave Posner met her and her friend, Becky Matthews, in a 7-Eleven parking lot on Mother's Day 1989 and quickly put them at ease.

"He sort of drew you into him and evoked your trust," she told the jury.

Dave took her out on his boat the next day and raped her.

Bradley broke down in tears while telling details about the

rape, and Judge Schaeffer had the jury removed from the courtroom while she regained her composure.

When asked whether she recognized "Dave" in the courtroom, Bradley did not hesitate.

"Right there," she said, pointing at Chandler.

~

Chandler's version of how he met Jan Bradley and Becky Matthews differed from what they told investigators. He told his attorney that it was actually Jan and Becky, rather than Chandler, who initiated conversation at the 7-Eleven. Chandler said that Jan was wearing tight-fitting clothes, a tube top, and cut off shorts. She was "pretty loaded" from drinking and kept "bumping up against him." She never objected to Chandler touching her body, including her breasts, and he could tell by the way she acted that she "was somebody that you could sleep with." Nevertheless, Chandler would not testify about his version of events at trial due to Zinober's legal strategy of treating the rape case and the Rogers murder case as two distinct and unrelated events.

TWENTY-ONE

After the prosecution finished presenting its case in chief, Zinober's defense team moved for a judgment of acquittal based on a lack of evidence supporting premeditated murder. The lead prosecutor seemed incredulous in his response:

> I believe there is overwhelming evidence of premeditation. I can't recall a case I've been involved in where it was clearer than this where three women are taken, tied up, had a ligature with a weight around their neck, and thrown into the water either to suffocate by the ligature or drown. There can be no other conclusion than the attempt was to kill the three ladies and eliminate them.

Judge Schaffer agreed and denied the motion, calling the

defense's contention of no evidence of premeditation "quite a stretch of the imagination."

In an effort to cast doubt into the minds of the jury members as to Chandler's guilt, Zinober called Dorothy Lewis, who had worked as a salesperson at Maas Brothers in Tampa's Westshore Mall just off I-275 in June 1989. Lewis testified that she saw Joan, Michelle, and Christe Rogers while working in the Juniors department of the store. According to Lewis, the store opened at 10:00 a.m. and the Rogers trio came in about twenty minutes later. When Lewis asked Joan if they needed any help, she replied that they just wanted to look around. They took several items of clothing to try on and Michelle asked Lewis to hold one garment for her, telling her that Maas Brothers was one of the first places they had been to in Tampa.

About 45 minutes later, they returned and purchased the garment. While Lewis rang up the sale at a cash register, Joan asked her for directions to Clearwater, and shortly afterward a man wearing a baseball hat walked up to them with a young child. He showed Christe a package before talking to Joan, then he asked Lewis if there was a children's department and she directed him to the second floor. The three Rogers women then followed him up the escalator. All five of the people seemed to be together, which surprised her because one of the girls had told her shortly before the man arrived that the three of them were traveling by themselves.

The defense also called Jeffrey Gaines, who testified that in June 1989 he worked as a bus boy at Sweden House Smorgasbord, which was part of the Gateway Inn hotel off

International Drive in Orlando. While working at the restaurant he encountered the Rogers trio, and when Michelle asked him for recommendations about where to go while they were in Orlando, he suggested that they visit Epcot Center. On a different day, he recalled seeing Joan sitting alone with a man at a table, but that man had his back to Gaines so he never got a good look at him.

Another defense witness, Officer Richard Pemberton of the Tampa Police Department, testified that on June 8, 1989 – the day that Joan Rogers's car was found at the Courtney Campbell Causeway boat ramp – he pulled a car over at that location and the Rogers vehicle was not there. He had pulled a car over at that location the day before as well, and the Rogers car was not there at that time either, nor did he believe it was there on June 5th or June 6th. Pemberton's partner, Kenneth Brogdon, testified similarly, confident that, on June 7, Joan Rogers's car had not been in the location where it was found on June 8.

Special Agent Wayne Oakes of the FBI's Hairs and Fibers Unit testified that he oversaw a trace evidence search of Chandler's boat and no hairs from Joan, Michelle, or Christe were found on it. However, that search did not occur until 1992, nearly three years after Chandler had sold the boat to someone else. On cross-examination, Oakes admitted that he was not surprised that no hairs from any of the victims were recovered after that passage of time.

To counter the testimony of the three inmates who testified for the prosecution, Zinober called two inmates of his own. Dave Rittehouse and Garland Stidham, who had shared a cell with Chandler, testified that they never heard him say anything about the Rogers murders despite the fact that investigators tried to coax them into saying he did by promising them special treatment in exchange for their cooperation.

Ileano Capo testified that she hired Chandler to do an aluminum screen job and that when she handed him a check around 7:15 a.m. on June 2, she did not notice any scratches or bruises on him and he did not seem to be acting nervous in any way. However, his hair was "all messed up" and "kind of looked like a clown's hair."

Yet another defense witness, Gayle Downey, stated that while staying at the Days Inn at Rocky Point on May 31, 1989, she saw a man on the second floor of the hotel walking toward her with a cooler. He was about 5'10", medium build, brownish, sun-bleached hair, about thirty years old, and attractive. Downey watched him walk to a light-colored boat with a blue strip on a trailer in the parking lot, and the trailer was attached to a black or dark blue Bronco or Blazer.

Zinober hoped the array of defense witnesses would create reasonable doubt in the juror's minds about Chandler's culpability for the murders of Joan, Michelle, and Christe. But the most important defense witness was yet to come.

TWENTY-TWO

On September 27, the eighth day of trial, more than 100 spectators packed Courtroom M to see Oba Chandler take the witness stand in his own defense. Most criminal defense attorneys believe that allowing the defendant in a murder trial to testify is a risky venture that unnecessarily exposes the defendant to damaging cross-examination by the prosecution. However, Fred Zinober preferred to have his clients testify whenever they denied guilt in a case. He had won half of his criminal cases following that strategy, so he saw no reason to change his approach with Oba Chandler.

Zinober believed that the only way Chandler could convince the jury to acquit him of the murder charges was by taking the stand, telling the jury how he only briefly met the victims, and explaining what he was doing the night of the murders. Zinober knew that the phone records putting

Chandler out on his boat in Tampa Bay on the night of the murders was a crucial piece of evidence. In the strategic reasoning of Zinober's legal mind, if his client could explain to jurors why he was out in his boat that night, it might be enough to get an acquittal.

Wearing a dark-blue blazer and dark tie, blue shirt, and khakis, the triple-murder defendant talked about living on Dalton Avenue with his wife, Debra, and daughter, Whitney, and working as an aluminum contractor building screen rooms and pool enclosures. He met Debbie when she worked as a sale representative for Alumco Industries, and they married about a year later. He owned several different boats while living there, but in June 1989 he owned a twenty-one-foot Bayliner that had a blue hull, white interior, and blue canvas top. After discussing more details about his aluminum contractor work, Zinober shifted his questioning to Chandler's meeting with the three Rogers women at a gas station on 50th Street off I-4.

> **Zinober**: Did there come a time during the course of that day that you met some people that you have subsequently learned to be Joan, Christe, and Michelle Rogers?
>
> **Chandler**: At that time, I only met Michelle, and I didn't really meet Christe. Christe was hanging out of the car. I never met Joan.
>
> **Zinober**: Why don't you tell us the circumstances of you meeting these people.

Chandler: Well, I don't recall exactly what time it was, but I know I was coming back off an estimate, and I stopped at a gas station on 50th and I-4. And when I pulled in, I went to get cigarettes and came back out, and she asked me –

Zinober: Who is "she"?

Chandler: I'm sorry. Michelle asked me if I knew where the Days Inn on 60 was. Well, I just proceeded to turn around, because there is a Days Inn right there. And 60 is a couple blocks down from where they was at.

And I just turned around and said, "There is the sign." And Christe stuck her head out hollering, "Rocky Point. Rocky Point."

I says, "You don't want this one; you want the one on Courtney Campbell Causeway."

So I just gave them directions, and that was it. I mean, nothing spectacular about it. I mean, total conversation, two minutes.

Zinober: And did you write directions?

Chandler: Yes, I did.

. . . . .

They was going to take 60, and I said, "no, get back up on the expressway here and go around."

. . . . .

It's a complicated intersection there. There's three or four lanes
that feed off into it. And I just told them, you know, "Go to the
light, hang a right, make a left back up on the Interstate, and
you're off and running."

Chandler estimated Michelle Rogers to be seventeen to
nineteen years old, and he thought she was "pretty." He wrote
the directions he gave her on the top of a brochure she had and
then they went their separate ways.

Zinober: Now, did you see these people again at any time
that day?

Chandler: I've never seen them again.

Zinober: Never saw them again in your life?

Chandler: No, sir.

Just in case the jurors did not understand the significance of
that testimony, Zinober asked him directly.

Zinober: Did you kill these people?

Chandler: No, I did not.

Zinober: Did you take them out on your boat?

Chandler: No, they've never been on my boat.

Chandler testified that on the night of the Rogers' disappearance, he was fishing at Gandy Bridge. He had gone out around 10:00 p.m. to "catch the tide changing" since that was the "best time to fish." When he started the boat's engine and pulled up the anchor, the engine died and he could smell gas in the bilge. He diagnosed the problem as a busted hose, which caused the bilge pump to bleed out all of the fuel from the gas tank. Then he explained how he had made it back to shore without any gas.

Zinober: Did assistance come?

.....

Chandler: The Coast Guard came by. I flagged them down, they said they'd come back to give me assistance if they could. And they couldn't. But another boat came by. I said, "Can you give me a tow to the marina?"

By that time, with daylight, I found out what my problem was, and I proceeded to tape my hose where it was leaking. And it didn't hold too well, but it did okay. Two guys gave me a tow to the Gandy Bridge Marina, and I got about five bucks of gas, and went back home.

Zinober finished his direct examination of Chandler with flair:

Zinober: Mr. Chandler, final question on this direct: Did you kill these ladies?

Chandler: I have never killed no one in my whole life. I have never – it's ludicrous. It's ridiculous.

During the prosecution's cross-examination, Chandler refused to answer any questions about the Madeira Beach rape case by invoking his Fifth Amendment privilege against self-incrimination. Crow purposely asked about the rape case over and over again, forcing Chandler to repeatedly plead the Fifth, which he did 21 times in total. Crow hoped that the jury would infer from Chandler's refusal to answer the questions that he was guilty of the rape. But Zinober was not concerned about the repeated reliance on the Fifth. It actually fell into his strategy. He believed that if the jurors became convinced that Chandler was going to be convicted in a separate trial on the rape charge, they would not feel as pressured to find him guilty in the murder case. Judge Schaeffer would later say that Zinober's strategy "bordered on brilliance."

When Crow switched to questions about the Rogers murders, Chandler asserted that he could not remember much detail about when he met the Rogers women:

Crow: Approximately what time did you meet them?

Chandler: I don't remember.

Crow: Give me your best estimate.

Chandler: Don't remember.

Crow: Was it morning?

Chandler: Don't remember.

Crow: Afternoon?

Chandler: Don't remember.

Crow: What were you doing?

Chandler: I don't remember, Mr. Crow.

Crow: Were you getting a contract?

Chandler: Pardon me?

Crow: What were you doing in the area?

Chandler: I am all over Tampa. I drive forty, fifty thousand miles around Tampa giving estimates and seeing about jobs, probably five, six hundred jobs a year that I do.

Crow: Okay. You have no idea what you were doing in that area?

Chandler: At that time, no. It was not a spectacular day for me.

As the cross-examination continued, Crow sparred with Chandler over many of his answers about how his boat broke down and when it had dawned on him that the three females he had given directions to were the Rogers women. Then Crow turned to another issue:

Crow: Did you flee the state?

Chandler: Yes, I did.

Crow: Because you were afraid?

Chandler: Because I was afraid of the Madeira Beach case, yes, I was.

Crow: You were just afraid of the beach case?

Chandler: That's right.

Crow: The connections to the homicide had nothing to do with it?

Chandler: Didn't worry me that much.

Crow sensed a chance to score some points with the jury and he jumped at the opportunity to use Chandler's response against him.

Crow: You weren't concerned about the fact that you were potentially identified in the Madeira Beach rape case and it just so happened that the police connected this with the Rogers case? The connection with the Rogers case didn't concern you?

Chandler: It worried me, but I figured you people would find out who did it.

Crow: Well, perhaps we have, Mr. Chandler.

Judge Schaeffer scolded Crow for showboating, but it had been worth it. After a break in the proceedings, the chief prosecutor resumed his cross-examination by returning to a topic that he had previously inquired about earlier in the day: the broken fuel line that caused Chandler's boat to run out of gas.

Crow: And it's your testimony, as a result of this broken line, the entire gas tank leaked?

Chandler: Yes.

Crow: And emptied?

Chandler: Yes.

. . . . .

Crow: Where was the break?

Chandler: Where it [gas line] went to the gas tank.

Crow: Wherever that is on your boat, if that's not at the bottom of the tank, it would not have leaked out, would it?

Chandler: I have no idea.

Following some brief questioning by Zinober on re-direct, the defense rested its case.

One potential witness that the defense was not allowed to have testify was Donald Adkinson, who had shared a cell with Hal Rogers's brother, John, at Allen Correctional Institution in Lima, Ohio. Adkinson claimed that John Rogers told him that he had been involved in a drug and pornography ring, and that he had hired two men named "Dave" and "Rick" to kill Joan Rogers because she knew too much about his drug activities. According to Adkinson, Michelle and Christe had been killed simply because they witnessed their mother's murder. Judge Schaeffer refused to let Adkinson testify because police had already rejected his story on grounds it was inconsistent with the physical evidence.

"John Rogers is a red herring that's not going to come before this jury," the judge ruled.

~

On January 28, the prosecution presented its rebuttal witnesses. Edwin Ojeda, an inmate who shared a cell with Chandler in February 1993, testified that he heard Chandler say that "his biggest mistake was leaving the note in the car."

But another mistake by Chandler would prove to be just as big. Assistant State Attorney Glenn Martin had been watching the trial via video in another part of the courthouse. Martin owned a boat himself and something about Chandler's testimony regarding the fuel leak did not make sense to him. As Chandler continued testifying, Martin called James Hensley, an expert mechanic for the Florida Marine Patrol, and asked him to inspect the *Gypsy I* to see if Chandler's contention about the gas leak could be true.

After confirming his suspicion that the *Gypsy I* had an antisiphon valve, the state called Hensley to the stand to address the alleged fuel line leak on Chandler's boat, including Chandler's claim that he used duct tape to seal the leak. With Assistant State Attorney Robert Lewis handling the line of inquiry, the testimony that followed proved to be extremely damaging to the defense.

Lewis: Did you have occasion to examine the fuel line?

Hensley: Yes, sir.

. . . . .

Lewis: Have you ever had experience with duct tape around gasoline?

Hensley: Never had much luck with any kind of tape around gasoline.

Lewis: Why not?

Hensley: The fuel itself dissolves the tape.

Lewis: Won't hold?

Hensley: No.

Hensley also disputed that the boat's fuel would be completely emptied out the gas tank with a hose failure like the one Chandler described.

Lewis: Does the fuel leak out then when there is a hole in the fuel line?

Hensley: Under current standards, it shouldn't, with the antisiphon valve which limits the loss of fuel from the tank into the bilge.

Lewis: How about this particular boat that you examined, is there an anti-siphoning valve in that?

Hensley: Yes, sir.

. . . . .

Lewis: If the fuel line were to rupture, break, get a pinhole in it, or fall apart, can fuel then come out of the tank and drain into the bilge?

Hensley: No, sir, not with that valve.

Lewis: What if this valve failed, if it didn't work?

Hensley: On this particular boat, it wouldn't make any difference, because the fuel lines and all the connections are above the top of the tank and eliminate any type of siphoning.

Hensley's testimony left Chandler visibly unsettled as he frantically sketched diagrams to show Zinober. On cross-examination, Zinober attacked Hensley's claim about the uselessness of duct tape to patch a broken fuel line.

Zinober: So are you saying you can't take duct tape and put it on there briefly and hold it together?

Hensley: I've never had any luck doing it.

Zinober: But it could be done, right?

Hensley: I would imagine.

. . . . .

Zinober: Best type of repair to keep two things together is tape, right?

Hensley: Not always around gasoline.

Zinober: Well, is there something better that you can think of to keep two things together if you have it?

Hensley: Clamps or two pieces of pipe. But you have to use whatever you have available.

Zinober: And if the only thing available was tape, you would tape it up, right?

Hensley: I imagine.

Sensing the damage caused by Hensley's testimony, Zinober

requested permission from the judge to call a rebuttal witness on the issue of the fuel line, claiming that he was surprised by the state's act of calling Hensley as a witness. In response, the lead prosecutor pulled no punches: "Judge, it seems to me that what happened is Mr. Zinober made the mistake of perhaps taking the accuracy of his client's statements without checking it out; and if there is a trap, he's caught in it because of his client's own making."

"Fred was trapped by his own client's lies and there was really nothing he could do to dig himself out again," Crow later commented.

TWENTY-THREE

On September 29, having completed all of the witness testimony, the parties proceeded to deliver their closing arguments to the jury. Speaking first, lead prosecutor Doug Crow discredited the defense's attempt to inject a phantom suspect as the murderer. He pointed out a credit card receipt that proved Joan Rogers was in the lobby of the Gateway Inn in Orlando at 10:02 a.m. on June 1, and thus could not possibly have been in Maas Brothers in the Westshore Mall in Tampa by 10:20 a.m. that day as defense witness Dorothy Lewis claimed. Crow also reminded the jury that although Joan Rogers "saved virtually every receipt" during her family's Florida vacation, there was no Mass Brothers receipt found among their belongings and no Maas Brother shopping bag or garment.

Crow cast Chandler's testimony as calculated and contrived: "The best way to sum up Mr. Chandler's testimony is he admits the obvious, he lies about the unknown, and he forgets the rest." He used "half-truth, half-lie" to tell a "convincing tale" and gain his victims' trust. He was a "chameleon-like person" who could "one minute portray the ingratiating Samaritan" and then suddenly become a "brutal rapist or conscienceless murderer."

Although Chandler asserted the Fifth Amendment with respect to any questions about the Madeira Beach rape case, Crow insisted that the jury should keep that case very much in mind:

> You got to take that rape case that happened eighteen days before this murder and you got to kind of hold it up and reflect it back and forth off the murder case. And what do you got? You got a situation where, through a chance meeting, he strikes up a conversation – the conversation in the rape case – talks about being from New York, close to the Canadian border, all that stuff, which we know is a bunch of baloney. Our situation . . . he had a conversation with them and gained their confidence and gained their trust.

> Both parties are tourists, new to the area, strange surroundings. Boat ride. Talks of his boat. Sells that as the contact point. You know. "Hey, boat ride. Go out in the boat." We know Blair went out in the boat. How do we know what Joan did? I suggest to you this evidence at the boat ramp in a car that says "blue-and-white boat." Makes no other sense.

. . . . .

Gained their confidence. Drew them to him. Set up a meeting. Rape case: Set up a meeting with Jan Bradley. This case: set up a meeting. Sunset cruise. And camera – "Bring your camera." Sunset cruise. "Sunsets are beautiful. Bring your camera."

. . . . .

Well, let's look at the murders. What can we reconstruct from these bodies? Well, we can tell you that duct tape was used and taped to their mouths. We can tell you that, although there were threats to kill in the rape case, he killed them in the murder case. And we can also tell you that they, like Judy, had their pants taken off. Missing their bottoms.

Striking similarities.

Then we know why Jan Bradley didn't lose her life. The only reason she's still around is because she had a lady waiting for her. That is the only difference in these cases. He had a witness out there who could identify him, in spite of the fact that he had used a false name.

After Crow finished, Zinober began his closing argument by emphasizing the premise that Chandler "is presumed innocent. And in this case, he's not only presumed innocent, but he got on the witness stand, and he told you people that, 'I am an innocent man. I did not do this crime. . . They have the wrong man.'" From there, Zinober focused on the state's burden of proving guilt beyond a reasonable doubt, insisting that such a burden had not been met. He also chose to highlight what he deemed to be Chandler's good character by reminding the jury that Chandler had stopped attempting anal sex with Jan Bradley when she pleaded that she had rectal cancer. Chandler had even apologized to Bradley afterward, implying that he felt remorseful about the rape and thus could not have committed three cold-blooded murders less than two months later.

> The State wants you to believe that this same person who she identified as Oba Chandler committed then, two weeks later, this monstrous act . . . . This act, what happened to Joan, Christe, and Michelle Rogers was a monstrous act. This was somebody that would be a monster. The person that committed that act on Joan, Christe, and Michelle Rogers would not have stopped performing anal sex because it hurt her and then said later on, "I'm sorry."

As Zinober wrapped up his closing argument, he urged the jury members to be mindful of not letting their emotions overcome reason when they viewed photographs of the Rogers' bodies. He reminded them to resist the urge of wanting to assign blame:

Ladies and gentlemen, it hurts to think that we'll never know what happened here. And we never will. We'll never know what happened to Joan, Christe, and Michelle Rogers . . . but if that's the way it's going to be, don't hang it on someone that didn't do it because someone has to pay.

During his rebuttal argument, in what would be the final word from the attorneys in the case, Crow countered the defense's contention that one man could not have subdued three women without having bruises or scratches on his face.

"They weren't controlled by brute force or a savage beating," Crow told the jury. "They were controlled by fear."

He called the boat a lure and a prison. It was both the thing that lured the victims to the scene of the crime and the thing that ensured they had no way to escape or get help. Once out at sea, Chandler had only to hold a knife to Christe or Michelle's throat, or a gun to their head, and tell Joan to lay down and submit if she wanted them to live.

"Any mother, any parent, will suffer any indignity, endure any pain, will place at great risk their own life to save the one thing that's most precious to them on this planet; the life of their child," he said.

And the defense suggestion that Chandler's moments of humanity in the rape case somehow precluded him from being the monster that killed the Rogers women should be dismissed outright. Rather than exculpating or exonerating Chandler, Crow contended that the rape should be seen as a stepping stone or building block for the murders.

He was mentally and morally prepared to commit the crime at the time he met the Rogers women. He had thought about it . . . . Those decisions are not made without some degree of preparation. And you know that eighteen days earlier, he came awful close. He had thought it out. He had rope. He had a knife . . . and he had three concrete blocks stored in his boat ready to do the deeds.

~

After hearing ten days of trial testimony, the jury deliberated for only 80 minutes before returning its unanimous verdict of guilty on all three counts of first-degree murder. Chandler showed no emotion as the court clerk read "guilty of murder in the first degree" three times. After being fingerprinted, Chandler smiled and thanked the bailiff who had handed him a paper towel to clean his hands.

Watching from the courtroom gallery, Jan Bradley noticed Chandler's lack of reaction as the three guilty verdicts were read.

"He seemed more like a monster sitting there, so still, without any flicker of emotion on his face," she said.

A member of the jury later revealed that the guilty verdicts were reached after just one vote and it had taken the jury only ten minutes to agree on the verdicts. The rest of the 80 minutes had been necessary because the jurors were so upset and emotional that they needed time to compose themselves before returning to the courtroom.

During the subsequent four-hour sentencing hearing, the prosecution presented evidence of Chandler's past crimes, including testimony from victims of the September 1992 jewelry robbery in Clearwater and the September 1976 home invasion robbery in Daytona Beach.

Assistant State Attorney Jim Hellickson, emphasizing the barbaric method of the Rogers murders, urged the jury to conclude that Chandler "deserves to pay the ultimate price." Hellickson told the jury that forensic examinations indicated that Chandler had killed Joan Rogers first, followed by Christe, and then Michelle. The execution had been carried out in such a monstrous fashion that it was difficult to even imagine it.

> It means two were alive, two were bound hand and foot while the other watched. Two people were watching, hearing, smelling what was happening at that point. Each knew they were going to be next because they were watching.

Chandler flatly rejected Zinober's plan to call Chandler's mother, his wife, son, and five-year old daughter to testify in support of life imprisonment over the death penalty. He did not want any members of his family testifying on his behalf.

"I've made a decision, your honor, to call no one," Chandler informed the judge.

"Do you understand that could be a mistake?" she asked.

"Yes, I do," he replied.

His hands metaphorically tied by his own client, as mitigating factors Zinober could only point to courses

Chandler took while in prison and phone records showing that Chandler called his mother from jail 85 times in one month.

"As long as there's love that's still alive, life should go on," Zinober told the jury.

Not surprisingly, the scales of justice dipped heavily against Chandler on the issue of an appropriate punishment for his crimes. It took the jury only 30 minutes to recommend the death penalty. Afterward, their duty done, jurors pointed to Chandler's own testimony as a major factor in their guilty verdict.

"His testimony damaged him very much," said juror Evelyn Calloway.

"He should have stayed off the stand," agreed Patricia Pittman.

"He made it very easy. Everything he said was a lie," Mary DeVault stated, referring to Chandler's testimony about his boat's fuel leak. "I'm no mechanic, but even I knew what he was saying was wrong."

Juror Roseann Welton put it in even stronger words.

"He scared some of the jurors when he would sit there and stare at you and have that stupid grin on his face," she said. "He would make your skin crawl. He had that smirk. I just wanted to walk over there and slap it off his face."

TWENTY-FOUR

Sentencing took place on November 4, 1994. Seven of the jury members who had found Chandler guilty drove back to Clearwater for the sentencing hearing and sat together in the front row of the courtroom. In determining the appropriate sentence, Judge Schaeffer considered various aggravating factors, including that the crime was especially heinous, atrocious, or cruel.

Imagining the horrific nature of the Rogers' murders left no doubt in the judge's mind about the cruel nature of the crime:

> Strangulation with a rope on board the Defendant's boat before each victim was thrown into the dark waters of Tampa Bay is the absolute best we can hope for, for each victim. Imagine the fear and anxiety of each victim with her hands and feet tied, her mouth bound by tape and rope around her neck

being pulled tight until blessed unconsciousness takes over. That would be heinous, atrocious, or cruel.

. . . . .

[T]he probable scenario is that this mother and her two daughters were lured aboard the Defendant's boat for a sunset cruise and picture taking. But after sunset they were taken against their will into the dark night on the then dark water aboard Chandler's boat.

He tied their hands behind their back to gain control. He taped their mouths to quiet their screams of terror. He removed their clothes and some sort of sexual assault occurred to one or all the victims. Then, Chandler put a rope around each victim's neck and tied the rope to a concrete block and then Chandler threw each victim, Joan, Michelle, and Christe Rogers overboard, alive, one by one, into the waters of Tampa Bay, where each died from drowning or from the block causing the rope to tighten around her neck or from a combination of drowning and strangulation.

The scene Judge Schaeffer described next would never be forgotten:

One victim was first; two watched.
    Imagine the fear.

One victim was second; one watched.

Imagine the horror.

Finally, the last victim, who had seen the other two disappear over the side, was lifted up and thrown overboard.

Imagine the terror.

Chandler's torture of these three women was over, but their panic and fear in the water before their merciful death is unfathomable.

Considering such immeasurable cruelty, any mitigating factors could not carry much weight. The judge acknowledged that Chandler's father committed suicide when he was ten years old, but noted that if Chandler experienced any abuse or neglect he "voluntarily elected not to present any evidence of it" and likewise chose not to have his psychologist testify on his behalf.

Chandler stood up from his seat at the defense table to hear the court impose the sentence of death for each of the three murders:

This Court agrees with the jury that in weighing the aggravating circumstances against the mitigating circumstances, the scales of life and death tilt unquestionably to the side of death.

Oba Chandler, you have not only forfeited your right to live among us under the laws of the State of Florida, you have forfeited your right to live at all . . . May God have mercy on your soul.

After the sentencing hearing, some of the jurors talked about the emotional impact that hearing about the horrific murders had on them.

"It was kind of disturbing," said Evelyn Calloway. "Those thoughts stuck in my mind, and a couple of nights I had nightmares."

Linda Jones, who had served as foreperson of the jury and became afraid of people and withdrawn following her experience of the trial, expressed her sentiments supporting Chandler's sentence of death.

"They need to do this swiftly," she said as her eyes teared up. "The man is a mutation of a human being and he needs to be destroyed."

There was one spectator who remained silent about the sentencing. He sat in a back corner of the courtroom. Having heard imposition of the sentence, Hal Rogers slipped out the door to make his way back home to Ohio.

TWENTY-FIVE

Though he had received his sentence in the Rogers case, Chandler's time in front of trial judges was not over. On October 13, 1994, Chandler faced trial for the March 1991 robbery of Sally Wurmnest. Prosecutors contended that after casing her jewelry booth at a local flea market, Chandler had followed her to her Blue Surf Condo home in Daytona Beach Shores. There he grabbed Wurmnest in the condo's underground parking lot and bound her with duct tape and wire ties.

Wurmnest testified that the robber had bound her eyes, mouth, and legs with duct tape and threatened to cut off her finger if she did not give him the ring she was wearing. He also stole $150,000 in jewelry, $16,000 in cash, a .38-caliber Smith & Wesson handgun, and her 1985 Dodge van. Fingerprints found on duct tape left behind at the crime scene matched those of

Chandler. However, in yet another instance of truth often being stranger than fiction, the jury acquitted Chandler of the crime.

The reason?

Wurmnest testified that her attacker had freckles on the back of his hands, but Chandler's hands had no such freckles.

~

The following February, Chandler's daughter, Kristal Mays, and his sister, Lula Harris, appeared on the *Maury Povich Show* along with Hal Rogers. Chandler himself also appeared, via videotape recorded at Union Correctional Institution in Raiford, Florida. Mays and Harris both acknowledged signing a $160,000 movie deal, but said they were donating their share to charity. Mays offered her share to Hal Rogers, but he turned it down. In his video statement, Chandler admitted "I'm not an angel," but insisted "I never hurt anybody" and called his accusers "liars, frauds, and thieves."

During a prison interview a few weeks later, Chandler told reporters that his last words whenever his death sentence was carried out would be: "Kiss my rosy red ass!" Asserting that his conviction would be overturned, he denied any fear of the possibility of his execution.

"I have no fear of it," he insisted. "If they kill me, they're going to be killing an old man. What am I supposed to do? Fall down and scream? This isn't my life. I've lived my life."

He voiced no regrets about his encounter with the Rogers women and what happened after that.

"Fate is fate," he said matter-of-factly. "There's nothing I can do to change things."

Chandler continued to claim that he had given Joan, Michelle, and Christe directions to their motel and then never saw them again.

"I just had the misfortune of meeting them," he explained.

He frowned when asked about relatives being paid in connection with a proposed movie about the murders.

"It's disgusting," he said with a look of disbelief, "making money off the death of a mother and two daughters."

Although he had adjusted to life on death row, he admitted that he missed fishing, a passion he attributed to his father who took him fishing every weekend as a boy until his suicide when Chandler was 10. He talked about getting to know many of the other inmates convicted of murder, just some of the over 350 in the state on death row. Reiterating his belief in fate, he claimed that most were "just natural, normal people that got caught up in something that turned their lives around." At no time did he express any remorse about what happened to Joan, Michelle, and Christe.

~

On April 2, 1995, the St. Petersburg Police Department determined that four women would share the $25,000 reward offered in the

Rogers case. Jo Ann Steffey was awarded $15,000; Steffey's sister was awarded $5,000 for calling the police on Steffey's behalf; while Mozelle Smith and her daughter Betty Curtis were given $2,500 each. Not long after the checks arrived in the mail the four women began bickering about who deserved what amount, while downplaying the roles the others had in identifying Chandler. Their rancor did not go unnoticed by the police department.

"That whole reward system was set up to be a symbolic appreciation for people coming forward," said spokesman Bill Doniel. "Now there's all this greed over the money. It's awful."

∼

As Chandler's appeals slowly wound their way through state and federal courts, he sat on death row for nearly two decades, his room and board paid for all the while by Florida taxpayers. But eventually, his time ran out.

On October 10, 2011, Florida Governor Rick Scott signed a death warrant for Chandler, scheduling his execution for 4:00 p.m. on November 15. The common reaction from those familiar with the case reflected the general sentiment that it was about time.

"I'm sorry that it's taken so long," said retired St. Petersburg Detective Cindra Cummings. "And I'm sorry he's not going to suffer the way they did." The Rogers family murders had left a lasting impact on her and she still thought of the three women whenever she drove over one of the bridges spanning Tampa Bay.

"He's finally going to pay the ultimate price," said J.J. Geoghegan, now a retired investigator. "I have no pity on him. It's been 18 years since he was convicted, and I've been waiting for this. If they would let me, I'd sit in on the execution."

"He was a real charmer," said Geoghegan, who was a St. Petersburg police detective at the time. "Back then, he was a good-looking man and a slick talker. He was a Ted Bundy, is what he was."

Longtime reporter Sue Carlton called it a "fitting end for a singular monster," deeming Chandler a "fresh horror" in the state that had also served as home to serial killers Ted Bundy, Danny Rolling, and Oscar Ray Bolin.

When Hal Rogers heard that Chandler's execution had been set, he went onto the Florida Department of Corrections website to look-up the man who had killed his wife and two daughters. He was a bit surprised when he came across Chandler's online mugshot. The face that seemed to look back at him over the internet was not the fierce monster he expected.

He just looks like a harmless old Charlie Brown, don't he?, Rogers thought. *Look at that picture. He looks just like someone's grandpa.*

Bruce Bartlett, Chief Assistant State Attorney at the prosecutor's office that helped convict Chandler, planned to attend his execution because of the egregiousness of the crime and his total lack of remorse.

"If Florida is going to have a death penalty, this individual is the poster child for having it," Bartlett said. "No matter what we do to him, it can't equal what he put those three victims through."

However, two of Chandler's children maintained their belief in his innocence, pointing to the lack of any direct evidence that he had committed the crimes.

"He may have been a con man, but he ain't a murderer," said Chandler's son, Jeff. "Can you imagine if you gave someone directions to their hotel and that's the only evidence you have against somebody? It was all circumstantial evidence. Show me some DNA, give me an eye-witness, show me something better than what was presented."

"There wasn't any forensic evidence," echoed Chandler's daughter, Valerie Troxell. "He gave them directions. They had a palm print. That's all they had."

The logistics of the crime convinced her that her dad could not have committed it.

"I don't think one person could have pulled off such a heinous crime. It would have to have been more than one person. I believe the killers are still out there."

TWENTY-SIX

On the day of his execution, November 15, 2011, Chandler ate his last meal at 10:00 a.m. It consisted of two salami sandwiches on white bread with mustard, a peanut butter and jelly sandwich on white bread, iced tea, and coffee. Some oppose the idea of allowing condemned death row inmates to choose their last meal. However, the courtesy of doing so is meant to affirm individuality and afford some dignity to the inmate during his final hours. Requests for last meals vary from individual to individual, but certain requirements ensure that the privilege is not abused. Whatever the requested last meal consists of, it must cost no more than $40, it must be purchased locally, and it must be prepared at the prison.

Among the group of witnesses who gathered in the execution chamber's small viewing room to see justice done,

Hal Rogers sat dressed in a grey pinstripe suit and vest, pink shirt, and tie. Hal had not planned on attending the execution until he learned that Mandi Scarlett, Michelle and Christe's cousin, would be going. He did not want her to go alone, so now he sat next to her in the center of the front row. They faced a large window shrouded by a brown curtain and sat silently for a while, each wondering what would happen. Although stoic on the outside, Hal secretly worried that Chandler might say something spiteful for his last words, something hateful meant to hurt his victims' family more.

At 4:07 p.m., the brown curtain rose and Hal saw Chandler strapped to a gurney. The 65-year-old convict was suffering from coronary artery disease, high blood pressure, and failing kidneys. Described by his appellate lawyer as a "broken man," Chandler had grown weary of prison life and resigned himself to his fate, though he still refused to take responsibility for the Rogers murders or express any remorse for their deaths.

Now, laying on his back with a white sheet covering him except for his face, Chandler's eyes were closed and intravenous tubes lead into both of his arms. When asked whether he had anything he wished to say, Chandler briefly opened his eyes and defiantly grumbled, "No."

At the appointed time, the execution team started the lethal injection machine. As the anesthetic seeped into his veins, Chandler's fingers fidgeted for a few moments, then stopped. Within a few minutes, his mouth hung open as if deep in sleep. At 4:14 p.m., the death cocktail itself began to flow, paralyzing him and then quietly stopping his heart.

The prison doctor pronounced him dead at 4:25 p.m.

Although he had banned members of his family from attending the execution and he declined to say any last words, Chandler did leave a "Last Statement" that he prepared seven hours earlier on a piece of notebook paper. The handwritten statement said simply: *You are killing an innocent man today.*

Perhaps Chandler believed that by maintaining his innocence he might still gain some last-minute reprieve.

Perhaps there was some part of him, no matter how small, that was good, and as the father of daughters himself, that good part still refused to believe that he could have committed such a brutal act to a mother and her two young daughters.

Perhaps that sliver of goodness is what caused him to vomit over the side of the boat when he realized what he had done after raping Jan Bradley a few weeks prior to the Rogers murders.

Perhaps he was, as he contended, wrongfully convicted, but that possibility is so small as to be virtually nonexistent.

One thing can be said with certainty: the 'y" of "today" in his final statement matched that of the handwriting on the Clearwater Beach brochure that had been so crucial in convicting him.

None of the jurors who had recommended the death penalty during Chandler's murder trial expressed any regret about their decision. However, the emotional wounds of that trial were reopened by Chandler's execution, and after his death some of the jurors reflected on how the trial had changed them.

"I've never owned a gun before," Roseanne Welton revealed. "I made my husband get me one after the trial."

"It made me look at people differently," agreed James Casey.

"I believe everybody who was in that jury room will go with a piece of them missing," said Don Fontaine. "We just clutch our kids really tight. There are other Oba Chandlers out there."

~

Outside the prison, Mandi Scarlett, niece of Joan Rogers, spoke to a gathering of reporters on behalf of the Rogers family.

"The family of Jo, Michelle, and Chris are very appreciative of everyone that has brought us to this day. The journey has been difficult for all of us involved," Scarlett said. She glanced across the street and saw Hal Rogers standing alone.

"Now is the time for peace," she said solemnly.

TWENTY-SEVEN

The fact that Oba Chandler convinced otherwise wary women to trust him enough to go on a boat ride at night within a few hours of meeting him seems incredulous. But we must remember the context. Though incomprehensible when imagined now in a time and place remote from the events, the trust that Chandler elicited from his victims in the 1980s is understandable given the combination of cunning, charisma, and charm he employed to make them feel comfortable and safe.

As Detective Glen Moore observed, Chandler "did very well at making people feel at ease."

~

At the time of his execution, Chandler had been on Florida's Death Row for 17 years, much longer than the average length of stay of 12.9 years. Similarly, the 22.5 years between Chandler's execution and his offense greatly eclipsed the average of 14.1 years.

Debra Chandler divorced Oba after his conviction for the Rogers killings and she cut him off from any contact with their daughter, Whitney.

No friends or family visited Chandler during his 17 years in prison.

After his death, his son claimed his body.

∽

James Hensley, the marine mechanic whose trial testimony caught Chandler in a lie, or at least fatally discredited him in the eyes of the jury, died of cancer just months after the conclusion of the trial.

∽

To keep their memory alive, the Rogers' family and friends established the Joan, Michelle, and Christe Rogers Memorial Fund to be used as an agricultural scholarship for a student from Van Wert County.

∽

Hal Rogers eventually remarried, starting a new life with a widow and her four children. They now have grandchildren together, but he will always have a hole in his heart from the loss of Joan, Michelle, and Christe.

"There is never returning to normal," he said. "There never is back to normal. It never goes away. It's always there somewhere."

~

In 2018, Chandler's daughter, Kristal Mays, posted about her father on weremember.com:

> I had hoped after his release from prison and marriage to Debra Whiteman, birth of Whitney Ann Chandler, that he had changed. He became worse. Hal Rogers, I pray you have peace. May GOD forgive Oba for his own soul's sake.

On September 14, 2020, poster Scars Angelspit, added:

> What you did to those poor women was unthinkable! I can't imagine the sheer terror they felt when you were doing what you did to them and as they sank into their watery graves, not being able to get a breath and unable to help one another.

> I can only hope you feel that same terror for your eternity.

I do not believe that four women were the only ones you raped and murdered. I think you were a serial killer and that more murders will be linked to you.

God may have mercy on your soul, but I doubt that's where you went.

But another visitor to the site, Caroline Williamson, took a different view, posting on August 8, 2021:

I truly feel that Mr. Chandler is not the murderer of the Rogers women. Too many reasons to list here. It was not him. About the other suspected murders attributed to him, I am not sure. This one case I'm sure about. It was not Oba Chandler. I always think that what if his Dad had not died in that basement that awful day. I believe his life would have turned out most positive and worthy. It really changed him. He was an innocent man on the day he was murdered. Sad.

∾

Jan Bradley, the Canadian tourist whose trial testimony about her brutal rape was crucial to Chandler's murder conviction, moved on with her life. She is married and now has children of her own.

∾

Judge Susan Schaeffer died of lung cancer in 2016. Fred Zinober, who unsuccessfully defended Oba Chandler in the trial overseen by Schaeffer, called her "the best of the best." Five years earlier, in the days immediately following Chandler's execution, Schaeffer summed up her feelings about the convicted killer.

"It was the worst case, as far as a defendant without a saving grace, that I ever handled," she said. "He did not have a soul, or if he did, it was a black one."

"Oba Chandler was the vilest, most evil defendant I ever handled."

– Criminal Circuit Court Judge Susan Schaeffer

EPILOGUE

On February 25, 2014, investigators in Broward County, Florida, made a major announcement in a nearly 25-year-old homicide case. Newly discovered DNA evidence identified Oba Chandler as the man who had raped and strangled to death Ivelisse Berrios-Beguerisse in November 1990 in Coral Springs. Although forensic analysis at the time had failed to detect semen in swabs taken from Beguerisse's body, vast improvements in DNA testing technology over the intervening years made the DNA match possible.

In September 2013, aware of the technological advances, Coral Springs Police Department detectives revisiting the cold case decided to send the swabs taken from Beguerisse's body to the Broward Sheriff's Office Crime Lab for DNA analysis using current technology and techniques. Five months later on February 4, 2014, the Crime Lab notified detectives that a male

DNA profile had been obtained from semen found on swabs taken from Beguerisse's vagina. After entering that DNA profile in the CODIS database, a match came back for Oba Chandler.

Chandler had briefly become a suspect in the Beguerisse case after the Florida Department of Law Enforcement notified Coral Springs detectives back in November 1992 that Chandler had been arrested for the Rogers triple homicide. At the time of Beguerisse's murder, Oba and Debra Chandler lived at 11600 NW 33rd St in Sunrise, Florida. Chandler's residence was only 1.5 miles northeast of the north entrance of the Sawgrass Mills Mall, where Beguerisse was last seen alive.

Unknown to Coral Springs investigators, Oba and Debra Chandler abruptly left their Sunrise home within days of Beguerisse's murder and moved to Port Orange, Florida. Oba Chandler roamed the streets for two more years before his arrest in the Rogers family homicide.

About two weeks after the murder, Beguerisse's husband moved back to Mexico, having no reason to remain in Florida following her death.

"In Mexico they kill for a reason," he said shortly before leaving. "Here, they kill for no reason."

~

Besides the Madeira Beach rape in May 1989, the triple-homicide of the Joan, Michelle, and Christe Rogers in June 1989, and the murder of Ivelisse Berrios-Beguerisse in

November 1990, St. Petersburg Police detectives believe that Oba Chandler committed many other rapes and murders over a thirty-year span dating back to 1963.

One of the other unsolved murders Chandler is suspected to have committed is that of 43-year-old Linda Little, who went missing on October 11, 1991 in Daytona Beach. Little was last seen leaving a 7-Eleven near the beachfront around 2:00 a.m. riding a blue bicycle towards her apartment. One of her sisters believes she saw Chandler at Little's apartment complex a few days before she disappeared. Perhaps not coincidentally, Linda Little went missing on Chandler's birthday.

In September 2011, Chandler was ruled out in a 1982 case in which he had long-been considered a suspect involving a woman's body found floating about 25 miles off the coast of Anna Maria Island. The body was wrapped in an afghan blanket and tied to a concrete block.

New Port Richey resident Amy Hurst was 29 when she disappeared. She was reported missing in November 1982 by her sister, who told authorities she had not seen Hurst for three months. Authorities did not identify the body as Hurst until July 2011 when the Manatee County Medical Examiner's Office compared DNA from the body to a sample from Hurst's son. Investigators ruled Chandler out as a suspect after Hurst's husband, William Gary Hurst, confessed to killing his wife and dumping her body into the waters off the coast of New Port Richey.

∽

It remains to be seen whether more brutal crimes will be conclusively linked to Chandler.

"Chandler was a pretty sharp criminal as criminals go," Chief Assistant State Attorney Bruce Bartlett said. "He was good at covering his tracks."

Regardless of what cold cases might be connected to Oba Chandler in the future as DNA technology continues to improve, Glen Moore takes satisfaction in knowing that his task force – with some timely aide by members of the public – succeeded in getting a killer permanently off the streets.

"I believe he'd still be killing today," Moore said. "That's the way these guys work. They kill and they kill and they kill. Until somebody stops them."

Even as the sun goes down,
To end the light of day
It's rising on a new horizon
Somewhere far away.

– Unknown Author

SELECTED BIBLIOGRAPHY

1. *Cold Case Files.* "Bodies in the Bay" (2001).
2. *Crime Stories.* "Bodies in the Bay" (2014).
3. Davis, Don. *Death Cruise.* New York: St. Martin's (1996).
4. *Forensic Files.* "Water Logged" (Dec. 2010).
5. *On the Case with Paula Zahn.* "Murder at Sunset" (Jan. 22, 2012).
6. Osinkis, Alison. Clinical Description of Drowning. *National Aquatics Journal* (1986).
7. Ressler, Robert, Ann Burgess, John Douglas. *Sexual Homicide: Patterns and Motives.* Lexington: Lexington Books, 1988.
8. Samenow, Stanton. *Inside the Criminal Mind.* New York: Crown Publishers, 2004.
9. Thompson, Yayenia. Describing personal drowning experience. www.quora.com (2018).
10. Yunger, Sebastian. *The Perfect Storm,* 1997.

NOTE ON SOURCE MATERIALS

This book is the result of countless hours spent tracking down and analyzing original source materials including the trial transcript of *State of Florida v. Oba Chandler*, Criminal Case No. CRC92-17438 (Sept. 1994), Vol. I-XIII, which was obtained from the State of Florida archives and includes all of the witness testimony, as well as police reports and witness interviews in the Rogers family murder investigation by the Hillsborough County Sheriff's Office and St. Petersburg Police Department and the Ivelisse Berrios-Beguerisse murder investigation by the Coral Springs Police Department.

Original source materials were supplemented with hundreds of newspaper articles covering the cases from *The Tampa Bay Times*, *Orlando Sentinel*, and others, along with legal briefs filed in *Oba Chadler v. State of Florida*, Case No. SC11-2055 and *Oba Chandler v. State of Florida*, Case No. 84812. One excellent secondary source consulted was *Angels & Demons*, the Pulitzer Prize winning series of newspaper articles about the Rogers case by Thomas French, who reviewed 4,000 pages of police reports and interviewed Hal Rogers, detectives, and others involved in the case.

Dialogue quoted in this book comes either from direct statements made by the speakers or witness recollection of the pertinent events.

ABOUT THE AUTHOR

JT Hunter is a true crime author with over fifteen years of experience as a lawyer, including criminal law and appeals. He also has significant training in criminal investigation techniques. When not working on his books, JT is a college professor and enjoys teaching fiction and nonfiction in his creative writing classes.

JT is the bestselling author of *The Devil In The Darkness: The True Story of Serial Killer Israel Keyes*, *A Monster of All Time: The True Story of Danny Rolling - The Gainesville Ripper*, and *The Vampire Next Door: The True Story of the Vampire Rapist*.

You can learn more about JT and his other books at jthunter.org

ALSO BY J.T. HUNTER

TORTURED WITH LOVE: The True Crime Romance of the Lonely Hearts Killers

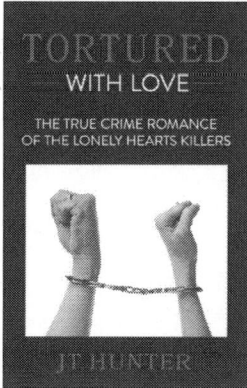

What is the price of passion? What is the power of love?

Meet Martha Beck, a young nurse dedicated to healing others, until her own hurting heart lured her down a darker path. Loneliness led her to Raymond Fernandez, but love led her all the way to the electric chair.

This is the tragic story of the Lonely Heart Killers.

❧

DEVIL IN THE DARKNESS: The True Story of Serial Killer Israel Keyes

He was a hard-working small business owner, an Army veteran, an attentive lover, and a doting father. But he was also something more, something sinister. A master of deception, he was a rapist, arsonist, bank robber, and a new breed of serial killer, one who studied other killers to perfect his craft. In multiple states, he methodically buried kill-kits containing his tools of murder years before returning and putting them to use. Viewing the entire country as his hunting grounds, he often flew to distant locations where he rented cars and randomly selected his victims. Such were the methods and madness of serial killer Israel Keyes. Such were the demands of the "Devil in the Darkness."

This book is the first detailed account ever published about Israel Keyes. It contains exclusive personal information about this frightening serial killer gleaned from extensive interviews with his former fiancee.

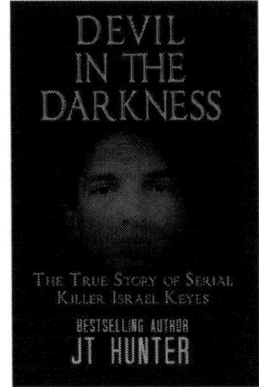

Optioned May 2018 by a Major Production company to be made into a motion picture.

~

A MONSTER OF ALL TIME: The True Story of Danny Rolling - the Gainesville Ripper

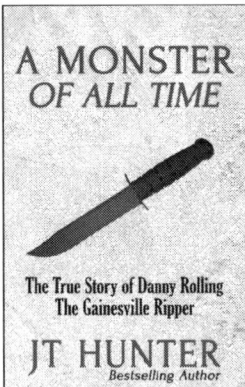

Ambitious, attractive, and full of potential, five young college students prepared for the new semester. They dreamed of beginning careers and starting families. They had a lifetime of experiences in front of them. But death came without warning in the dark of the night. Brutally ending five promising lives, leaving behind three gruesome crime scenes, the Gainesville Ripper terrorized the University of Florida, casting an ominous shadow across a frightened college town.

What evil lurked inside him? What demons drove him to kill? What made him "A Monster of All Time"?

~

IN COLDER BLOOD: On the Trail of Dick Hickock and Perry Smith

Two families, mysteriously murdered under similar circumstances, just a month apart. One was memorialized in Truman Capote's classic novel, *In Cold Blood*. The other was all but forgotten.

Dick Hickock and Perry Smith confessed to the first: the November 15, 1959 murder of a family of four in Holcomb, Kansas. Despite remarkable coincidences between the two crimes, they denied committing the second: the December 19 murder of a family of four in Osprey, Florida.

Over half a century later, a determined Florida detective undertakes exceptional efforts to try to bring closure to the long-cold case.

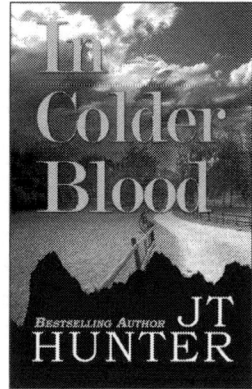

~

THE COUNTRY BOY KILLER: The True Story of Cody Legebokoff

He was the friendly, baby-faced Canadian boy next door. He came from a loving, caring, and well-respected family. Blessed with good looks and back-woods charm, he was popular with his peers and he excelled in sports. A self-proclaimed "die hard" Calgary

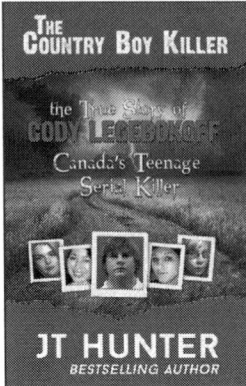

Flames fan, he played competitive junior hockey and competed on his high school's snowboarding team. And he enjoyed the typical pleasures of a boy growing up in the country: camping, hunting, and fishing with family and friends. But he also enjoyed brutally murdering women, and he became one of the youngest serial killers in Canadian history.

~

THE VAMPIRE NEXT DOOR: The True Story of the Vampire Rapist

John Crutchley seemed to be living the American Dream. Good-looking and blessed with a genius level IQ, he had a prestigious, white-collar job at a prominent government defense contractor, where he held top secret security clearance and handled projects for NASA and the Pentagon.

To all outward appearances, he was a hard-working, successful family man with a lavish new house, a devoted wife, and a healthy young son. But, he concealed a hidden side of his personality, a dark secret tied to a hunger for blood and the overriding need to kill.

As one of the most prolific serial killers in American history, Crutchley committed at least twelve murders, and possibly nearly three dozen. His IQ eclipsed that of Ted Bundy, and his body count may have as well. While he stalked the streets hunting his unsuspecting victims, the

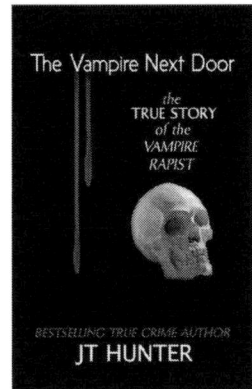

residents of a quiet Florida town slept soundly, oblivious to the dark creature in their midst . . . unaware of the vampire next door.

Printed in Great Britain
by Amazon